The
Indian
Vegetarian
Cookbook

The
Indian
Vegetarian
Cookbook

Compiled by
Master Chefs of India

Lustre Press
Roli Books

ISBN: 81-7436-169-3

© **Roli & Janssen BV 2000**
Second impression 2006
Published in India by Roli Books
in arrangement with Roli & Janssen
M-75 Greater Kailash II (Market)
New Delhi 110 048, India
Ph: ++91 (11) 29212271, 29212782
29210886; Fax: ++91 (11) 29217185
E-mail: roli@vsnl.com; Website: rolibooks.com

Cover: Sneha Pamneja
Layout: Kumar Raman
Front and back covers: Roli collection

Printed and bound by Press Tech Litho Pvt. Ltd., Noida, U.P.

Contents

Tastes of India

India is perhaps the only country in the world where vegetarian cooking actually has a tradition, and an ancient one at that! In a land so rich in cultural heritage, it is but natural that Indian cuisine is multifarious, delighting both the eye and the palate.

The range of vegetables used offer the gourmet scope for thousands of exciting recipes. This book presents a variety of vegetarian dishes cooked in different styles, ranging from tandoori and stir-fried to curries.

Tandoori food is extremely popular all over the world. It is a cuisine that suits the international palate, since it is lightly spiced, and easy to cook and serve. It derives its name from the *tandoor*, a large coal-fired oven, the modern alternatives of which are the oven, electrical grill or the microwave. While it is similar to barbecued food, tandoori cuisine has more delicate flavours, since it uses a variety of marinades and spices. Vegetarian tandoori preparations include an exciting array of dishes. Tandoori food may be served as starters, or form a part of the main course, accompanied by different kinds of Indian breads and yoghurt-based dishes.

Stir-fried cooking derives its name from the quick and easy technique used for the preparation of delicious Indian dishes. Spices dominate the contents, since they have a strong taste and fragrance which provide flexibility to the principal ingredient.

South Indians steam many of their preparations, as a result of which, every home is equipped with large and small steaming pots. In the north, however, people do not steam their food at all, though they use a technique known as *dum pukht* (cooking on low heat).

A large part of India is vegetarian. Not surprisingly, there are strong regional variations in the cuisine, which make for an exceptional richness and variety of flavours and preparations. Different regions in India offer their own specialities with their very own taste, subtlety and aroma. The country's vast reservoir of spices, made from its abundance of tropical herbs, flavours the food, and contains medicinal and preservative properties. Turmeric, for example, is an antiseptic, and can be used both internally and externally. Asafoetida is a digestive which combats flatulence. Garlic is good for circulatory ailments, coriander and tamarind for constipation, cloves for toning up the heart, and black pepper for giving energy.

Indian food is usually served with either steamed rice or unleavened bread, or both following each other in succession. In the north, wholewheat breads, such as chapatis and parathas, are commonly eaten, while in the south the preferred choice is plain rice. Traditional Indian breads are flat, baked on cast iron griddles. The Muslims introduced ovens where sour dough and plain breads, such as *naans*, could be baked.

At most Indian meals, besides vegetables, rice or bread, there are also relishes, yoghurt-based dishes, pickles and chutneys. They round off the full cycle of flavours and textures, adding bite, pungency and often vital minerals and vitamins as well.

Indian restaurants in different countries have fine tuned Indian recipes to suit local tastes. Easy availability of the various ingredients used in Indian kitchens, facilitates the preparation of Indian cuisine even at home.

A traditional Indian meal is a wholesome and delectable experience. Our selection of recipes ensures that you get the entire taste and texture of its preparation without fuss.

Basic Preparations

Garam masala powder: Take 18 gm each of black cumin (*shah jeera*) seeds and cumin seeds, 40 gm cloves (*laung*), 12 bay leaves (*tej patta*), 40 black cardamom (*badi elaichi*) seeds, 6 cinnamon (*dalchini*) sticks, 25 black peppercorns (*sabut kali mirch*), 1 gm mace (*javitri*) and 9 gm ginger powder (*sonth*).

Dry roast all the ingredients (except mace and dry ginger powder) on low heat until aromatic. Remove and cool. Mix all the roasted spices, mace and dry ginger powder and grind to a fine powder. Sieve and store in an airtight container.

Panch phoran: Mix equal quantities of fenugreek seeds (*methi dana*), cumin (*jeera*), fennel (*saunf*), mustard seeds (*rai*) and onion seeds (*kalonji*). Store in an airtight jar and use as and when required.

Tikki masala (spice cake): Dissolve 100 gm asafoetida (*hing*) in ½ cup water. Strain and add 100 gm black gram (*urad dal*) powder, 50 gm ginger powder (*sonth*), 100 gm red chilli powder, 50 gm aniseed (*moti saunf*) powder, 25 gm coriander (*dhaniya*) powder, 15 gm garam masala, 10 gm black cardamom (*badi elaichi*) powder, 10 gm cinnamon (*dalchini*) powder, 25 gm cumin (*jeera*) powder, 5 gm mace (*javitri*) powder, 5 gm nutmeg (*jaiphal*) powder, 10 gm clove (*laung*) powder, 5 gm black cumin (*shah jeera*) powder, 5 gm carom (*ajwain*) seeds, 100 ml oil and 150 ml water. Mix well and knead into a hard dough. Divide the dough equally into 20-25 portions and shape each into flat, round cakes. Place these on a greased tray and sun-dry for a day. Turn over and dry the other side also. When completely dry, store in airtight jars, and use as required.

Vegetable stock: Combine 4 carrots, washed and scrubbed; 8 whole spring onions; 6 outer lettuce leaves, 1 tsp salt and 1 lt water and bring to the boil. Cover, lower heat and simmer for ½ hour. Strain the stock through a muslin cloth and use as required.

Mustard paste: Wash 200 gm mustard seeds (*rai*) and grind to a paste by adding enough water to get a paste-like consistency.

Soups and Beverages

Mint-flavoured yoghurt soup

Prep. time: 20 min. • Cooking time: 30 min. • Serves: 4

Ingredients

Yoghurt (*dahi*)	2¾ cups / 495 gm
Water	2½ cups / 500 ml
Salt to taste	
Black pepper (*kali mirch*) powder	1 tsp / 2 gm
Cumin (*jeera*) powder, roasted	1 tsp / 2 gm
Lemon (*nimbu*) juice	2 tbsp / 30 ml
Cream (*malai*)	¾ cup / 150 gm
Mint (*pudina*) leaves, chopped	3 cups / 45 gm

Method

1. Heat the water in a pan and gradually blend in the yoghurt.
2. Add the salt, black pepper powder, cumin powder and lemon juice. Cook on low heat for 15 minutes.
3. Add the cream and mint leaves, stir and cook on low heat for 10 more minutes.
4. Remove from heat, pour the soups into individual bowls and serve hot.

Tangy and spicy tomato soup

Prep. time: 30 min. • Cooking time: 45 min. • Serves: 4

Ingredients

Tomatoes	800 gm
Vegetable oil	4 tbsp / 40 ml
Cinnamon (*dalchini*), 1" sticks	3-4 pcs / 5 gm
Cloves (*laung*)	5-6 pes / 5 gm
Bay leaves (*tej patta*)	2
Green cardamoms (*choti elaichi*)	4
Ginger (*adrak*), chopped	½ tbsp / 12 gm
Garlic (*lasan*), chopped	1 tbsp / 12 gm
Water	5 cups / 1lt
Salt to taste	
Black pepper (*kali mirch*) powder to taste	
Cream (*malai*)	⅓ cup / 60 gm

Method

1. Heat the oil in a deep pan; add all the whole spices and sauté till they crackle.
2. Add the tomatoes, ginger, garlic and water. Bring the mixture to the boil and cook on low heat for 30 minutes.
3. Remove from heat and mash the tomatoes. Strain the liquid through a soup strainer into another pan. Discard the tomato pulp.
4. Heat the soup, adjust the seasoning and remove from heat. Stir in the cream and serve hot.

Tomato soup flavoured with coconut

Prep. time: 15 min. • Cooking time: 30 min. • Serves: 4

Ingredients

Tomatoes, chopped	500 gm
Coconut (*nariyal*), grated	½ cup / 120 gm
Coconut oil	3 tbsp / 30 ml
Garlic (*lasan*), chopped	2 tsp / 6 gm
Onions, chopped	3½ tbsp / 40 gm
Ginger (*adrak*), crushed	1 tbsp / 24 gm
Salt to taste	
White pepper (*safed mirch*) powder	$\frac{1}{3}$ tsp / 1 gm
Bay leaves (*tej patta*)	4
Vegetable stock (see p. 8)	7 cups / 1½ lt
Cream (*malai*)	2 tbsp / 40 gm

Method

1. Heat the coconut oil in a pot; sauté the garlic and onions for a few seconds.
2. Add the coconut and stir-fry. Add the tomatoes and ginger.
3. Stir in the salt, white pepper powder, bay leaves and vegetable stock. Simmer for 15-20 minutes till the tomatoes are cooked and tender. Remove from heat and keep aside to cool.
4. Blend the mixture, strain through a muslin cloth and reheat. Remove from heat and stir in the cream.
5. Pour into individual soup bowls and serve immediately.

Spinach soup

Palak ka Shorba

Prep. time: 20 min. • Cooking time: 30 min. • Serves: 4

Ingredients

Spinach (*palak*), washed, finely chopped	500 gm
Butter	2 tbsp / 40 gm
Refined flour (*maida*)	2 tbsp / 30 gm
Ginger (*adrak*), chopped	5 tsp / 50 gm
Garlic (*lasan*), chopped	1 tsp / 3 gm
Black peppercorns (*sabut kali mirch*)	5-6
Bay leaves (*tej patta*)	4
Salt to taste	
White pepper (*safed mirch*) powder	a pinch
Vegetable stock (see p. 8)	7 cups / 1½ lt

Method

1. Melt the butter in a pot; add the refined flour and cook to a sandy texture.
2. Add the ginger, garlic, spinach and sauté for a few minutes. Add the black peppercorns, bay leaves, salt, white pepper powder and vegetable stock. Simmer for 15-20 minutes.
3. Remove the spinach from the stock and blend to a purée. Return the spinach purée to the stock and cook for 5 minutes.
4. Remove from heat, pour into individual soup bowls and serve hot.

Carrots blended with orange juice

Prep. time: 30 min. • Cooking time: 40 min. • Serves: 4

Ingredients

Carrots (*gajar*), cut into small cubes	500 gm
Orange (*santra*) juice	4 cups / 800 ml
Butter	5 tsp / 25 gm
Onions, chopped	$^2/_3$ cup / 160 gm
Salt to taste	
White pepper (*safed mirch*) powder	$^1/_3$ tsp / 1 gm
Sugar	$3^1/_3$ tbsp / 30 gm
Cream (*malai*)	½ cup / 100 gm

Method

1. Melt the butter in a pan; add the onions and sauté till transparent. Add the carrots and sauté for a minute. Add the remaining ingredients except cream and cook on low heat till the carrot is tender.
2. Remove from heat and then strain through a muslin cloth.
3. Reheat the strained soup and stir in the cream. Remove from heat, pour into individual soup bowls and serve hot.

Creamed broccoli garnished with walnuts

Prep. time: 15 min. • Cooking time: 40 min. • Serves: 4

Ingredients

Broccoli, cut into florets	400 gm
Butter	2 tbsp / 40 gm
Onions, chopped	2 tbsp / 24 gm
Garlic (lasan), chopped	1 tsp / 3 gm
Leeks, chopped	20 gm
Celery, chopped	20 gm
Salt to taste	
White pepper (safed mirch) powder	½ tsp / 1gm
Vegetable stock (see p. 8)	7 cups / 1½ lt
Cream (malai)	½ cup / 100 gm
Walnuts (akhrot), chopped	1 tbsp / 15 gm

Method

1. Heat the butter in a pot; add the onions and garlic, sauté for a minute. Add the leeks, celery, broccoli and stir-fry.
2. Stir in the salt, white pepper powder and vegetable stock. Simmer for 20 minutes until the broccoli is tender.
3. Remove the broccoli from the soup and keep aside to cool. When cool, blend to a purée. Mix the purée into the soup and strain through a muslin cloth.
4. Reheat the strained soup and stir in the cream.
5. Remove from heat, pour into soup bowls and serve hot garnished with walnuts.

Watermelon juice flavoured with mint

Prep. time: 30 min. • Serves: 4

Ingredients

Watermelon (*tarbuj*)   4.5 kg
Mint (*pudina*) leaves, chopped   1 tsp / 2 gm
Black rock salt (*kala namak*) to taste

Method

1. Cut the flesh of the watermelon into small chunks, discard the rind. Remove all the seeds.
2. Blend the watermelon chunks with mint leaves.
3. Strain through a muslin cloth and discard the pulp.
4. Serve chilled in individual glasses.

Paracetamol Power

*Fruit stains can be removed from your
clothes, if the area is rubbed with powdered
paracetamol tablets, and then washed with
warm soap water.*

Bael squash

Prep. time: 10 min. + overnight • Serves: 4

Ingredients

Bael (*bel*), large   1
Water   5 cups / 1 lt
Sugar, powdered   ½ cup / 100 gm

Method

1. Break open the bael and remove the pulp.
2. Soak the pulp in water and leave overnight.
3. Dissolve the sugar in the water and strain the mixture through a muslin cloth. Discard the pulp.
4. Serve chilled in individual glasses.

Fruity Cubes

Leftover syrup from canned fruits can be frozen in ice trays. Add a cube of frozen fruit syrup to lemon juice for flavour and taste.

Mango summer cooler

Prep. time: 15 min. • Cooking time: 30 min. • Serves: 2-4

Ingredients

Mangoes, raw, peeled, sliced	750 gm
Water	5 cups / 1 lt
Salt to taste	
Sugar	1 cup / 150 gm
Cumin (*jeera*) powder	1 tsp / 2 gm
Mint (*pudina*) leaves, finely chopped	1 bunch

Method

1. Boil the mangoes for ½ an hour. Remove from the flame and keep aside to cool.
2. Mash the mango to pulp and pass the mixture through a sieve.
3. Mix in the salt, sugar and cumin powder. Stir well till the sugar dissolves completely.
4. Serve chilled garnished with mint leaves.

Sweet and sour tamarind drink

Prep. time: 1 hr. • Serves: 2-4

Ingredients

Tamarind (*imli*), soaked in 1 cup warm water for 1 hour   1 cup
Water   4 cups / 800 ml
Sugar   1 cup / 150 gm

Method

1. Extract the pulp of the tamarind.
2. Add the water and sugar. Stir till the sugar dissolves completely.
3. Pass the mixture through a sieve. Serve chilled.

Fragrant Water

To add fragrance to drinking water, put rose
petals in the water jug. The water remains
fresh and smells sweet.

Millet flour in yoghurt

Prep. time: 15 min. • Cooking time: 3 hrs. • Serves: 4-6

Ingredients

Yoghurt (*dahi*)	1¾ cups / 325 gm
Millet flour (*bajra*)	4 tbsp / 32 gm
Butter	7 tsp / 35 gm
Ginger-garlic (*adrak-lasan*) paste	4 tsp / 24 gm
Water	15 cups / 3 lt
Salt to taste	
Cumin (*jeera*) seeds, roasted, powdered	1 tsp / 2 gm
Green coriander (*hara dhaniya*), chopped	1 tbsp / 4 gm

Method

1. Mix the yoghurt and millet flour in a bowl. Keep aside.
2. Heat the butter in a pan; add the ginger-garlic paste and sauté over medium heat for 2-3 minutes or until brown in colour.
3. Stir in the yoghurt mixture and bring to the boil.
4. Add water and simmer, till it is reduced to ²/₃rd the original quantity.
5. Add salt and mix well. Remove from heat and cool to room temperature. Pass the mixture through a muslin cloth.
6. Serve chilled garnished with cumin powder and green coriander.

Snacks and Starters

Cottage cheese and spinach kebabs

Prep. time: 30 min. ● Cooking time: 15 min. ● Serves: 4

Ingredients

Cottage cheese (*paneer*), grated	450 gm
Spinach (*palak*), boiled, blended	900 gm
Green cardamom (*choti elaichi*) powder	2 tsp / 4 gm
Cashew nuts (*kaju*)	½ cup / 60 gm
Green coriander (*hara dhaniya*), chopped	4 tsp / 20 gm
Garam masala (see p. 8)	4 tsp / 8 gm
Ginger (*adrak*) paste	3 tbsp / 35 gm
Gram flour (*besan*), roasted	¼ cup / 20 gm
Green chillies, chopped	15
Mace (*javitri*) powder	2 tsp / 4 gm
Salt to taste	
Vegetable oil for deep-frying	
Onion, medium-sized, cut into rings	1

Method

1. Mix all the ingredients (except oil and onion) together. Divide the mixture into lemon-sized balls and shape into 1½" -round patties.
2. Heat the oil in a frying pan; deep-fry the patties till golden brown. Remove with a slotted spoon and drain the excess oil on absorbent kitchen towels.
3. Serve garnished with onion rings as a snack or as an accompaniment with a rice and curry dish.

Succulent kebabs made with yoghurt

Prep. time: 2½ hrs. • Cooking time: 30 min. • Serves: 4

Ingredients

Yoghurt (dahi), hung	2 cups / 360 gm
Roasted gram (chana), powdered	½ cup / 50 gm
Salt to taste	
Red chilli powder	2 tsp / 4 gm
Clove (laung) powder	1 tsp / 2 gm
Green cardamom (choti elaichi) powder	½ tsp / 1 gm
Cinnamon (dalchini) powder	a large pinch
Black pepper (kali mirch) powder	½ tsp / 1 gm
Vegetable oil	½ cup / 90 ml
Garlic (lasan) paste	2 tsp / 12 gm
Onions, sliced, fried, ground	¼ cup / 30 gm
Milk	¼ cup / 45 ml

Method

1. Add the roasted gram, salt and half of all the spices to the hung yoghurt and mix well.
2. Divide the mixture into 20 equal portions. Flatten each portion to get a smooth, even shape.
3. Heat the oil in a pan; fry the kebabs, a few at a time, to a light golden colour. Keep aside.
4. In the same oil, add the salt, garlic paste, ground onions and the remaining half of the spices. Stir-fry for a few minutes. Add the kebabs and turn gently till each piece is coated with the mixture.
5. Pour milk over the kebabs and let the mixture sizzle for 10 seconds. Serve hot.

Lentil kebabs

Prep. time: 15 min. • Cooking time: 25 min. • Serves: 4

Ingredients

Lentil (*masoor dal*), washed	1½ cups / 240 gm
Water as required	
Green chillies, deseeded, chopped	2-3
Green coriander (*hara dhaniya*), chopped	2 tsp / 4 gm
Ginger (*adrak*), finely chopped	2 tsp / 25 gm
Salt to taste	
Red chilli powder	a pinch
Chaat masala	¾ tsp / 1 gm
Breadcrumbs (white)	3⅔ tbsp / 50 gm
Cornflour	1 tsp / 2 gm
Garam masala (see p. 8)	a pinch
Vegetable oil for frying	

Method

1. Boil the lentil in water till soft. Drain the excess water and mash the lentil with a wooden spoon.
2. To the mashed lentil, add the green chillies, green coriander, ginger, salt, red chilli powder, *chaat* masala, breadcrumbs, cornflour and garam masala. Mix well. Divide and shape the mixture equally into 16 medallions.
3. Heat the oil in a wok (*kadhai*); deep-fry the medallions until light brown. Remove with a slotted spoon and drain the excess oil on absorbent kitchen towels.
4. Serve hot.

Exotic lotus stem kebabs

Prep. time: 15 min. • Cooking time: 45 min. • Serves: 4

Ingredients

Lotus stems (*kamal kakri*), washed, chopped	900 gm
Bengal gram (*chana dal*), split and husked	1 cup / 160 gm
Chaat masala	2 tsp / 4 gm
Green coriander (*hara dhaniya*), chopped	4 tsp / 8 gm
Garam masala (see p. 8)	4 tsp / 8 gm
Green chillies, chopped	1/2 cup / 60 gm
Onions, chopped	1/3 cup / 80 gm
Red chilli powder	2 tsp / 3 gm
Roasted gram (*chana*), powdered	3 tbsp / 30 gm
Salt to taste	
Vegetable oil for frying	

Method

1. Boil the lotus stems in a pan with Bengal gram. Cook till tender and dry.
2. Grind the mixture to a thick paste without using any water.
3. Add the remaining ingredients except oil to the paste. Knead for 5 minutes. Divide the mixture equally into lemon-sized balls. Shape each ball into small cutlets and deep-fry in hot oil.
4. Serve hot with mint chutney (see p. 214).

Nadru Shami Kebab

Succulent kebabs cooked in yoghurt

Prep. time: 30 min. • Cooking time: 1 hr. • Serves: 4

Ingredients

Bengal gram (*chana dal*)	2 cups / 320 gm
Salt to taste	
Coriander (*dhaniya*) powder	1 tsp / 2 gm
Cumin (*jeera*) powder	1/2 tsp / 1 gm
Green chilli paste	3 tbsp / 45 gm
Onion paste	4 tbsp / 100 gm
Garlic (*lasan*) paste	5 tsp / 30 gm
Yoghurt (*dahi*)	1/2 cup / 90 gm
Vegetable oil	2 tbsp / 20 ml
Water	2 cups / 400 ml
Roasted gram (*chana*), powdered	5 tsp / 25 gm
Garam masala (see p. 8)	a large pinch
Sugar, powdered	1/2 tsp / 1 1/2 gm
Vegetable oil for deep-frying	

Method

1. Mix the Bengal gram with all the ingredients except roasted gram, garam masala, sugar and vegetable oil. Boil till it is tender and dry.

2. Grind the mixture to a thick paste without using any water. Mix in the remaining ingredients and knead till the dough is soft and smooth.

3. Divide the dough into lemon-sized portions. Shape each portion into round patties.

4. Heat the oil in a wok (*kadhai*); deep-fry the patties on low heat till golden brown.

5. Serve hot with mint chutney (see p. 214).

Melt-in-the-mouth turnip kebabs

Prep. time: 30 min. • Cooking time: $1\frac{1}{2}$ hrs. • Serves: 4

Ingredients

Turnips (*shalgam*), quartered	$1\frac{1}{4}$ kg
Onions, finely sliced	$\frac{1}{4}$ cup / 30 gm
Salt to taste	
Red chilli powder	$\frac{1}{2}$ tsp / 1 gm
Garam masala (see p. 8)	$\frac{1}{4}$ tsp / 1 gm
Roasted gram (*chana*), powdered	2 tbsp / 20 gm
Vegetable oil for shallow frying	

Method

1. Fry the onions in 1 tbsp oil till golden brown and crisp. Remove and grind coarsely.
2. Boil the turnips in water. When tender, take a few pieces of turnip at a time, wrap them in a muslin cloth and squeeze out as much liquid as possible.
3. Mash the turnips. Add the salt, red chilli powder, garam masala, roasted gram powder and the onions. Mix and knead well.
4. Divide the mixture into 8 portions. Flatten and shape each into patties with wet palms.
5. Heat the oil on a griddle (*tawa*); shallow fry the patties till golden brown.
6. Serve hot with *subz biryani* (see p. 198).

Cottage cheese kebabs coated with sesame seeds

Prep. time: 30 min. • Cooking time: 15 min. • Serves: 6

Ingredients

Cottage cheese (*paneer*), finely grated	500 gm
Green cardamom (*choti elaichi*) powder	1/2 tsp / 1 gm
Garam masala (see p. 8)	2 tsp / 4 gm
Green chillies, chopped	2
Green coriander (*hara dhaniya*), chopped	2 tsp / 4 gm
Mace (*javitri*) powder	1/2 tsp / 2 gm
Onions, finely chopped	1/2 cup / 120 gm
White pepper (*safed mirch*) powder	1 tsp / 2 gm
Yellow or red chilli powder	1 1/2 tsp / 2 gm
Yoghurt (*dahi*), drained	2 cups / 360 gm
Salt to taste	
Gram flour (*besan*) or cornflour	1/4 cup / 25 gm
Sesame (*til*) seeds	1/2 cup / 60 gm
Egg white (optional)	1
Vegetable oil	1/2 cup / 85 ml

Method

1. Mix all the ingredients till gram flour / cornflour with a wooden spoon for 2 minutes.
2. Divide this mixture equally into 20 balls. Compress each ball slightly to get a 4 cm round patty. Refrigerate the patties for 20 minutes.
3. Sprinkle some sesame seeds over the patties and shallow fry on a griddle until crisp and golden. Alternatively, you could lightly coat each patty with beaten egg white, before sprinkling sesame seeds and frying. Serve hot.

Yam kebabs

Prep. time: 20 min. • Cooking time: 20 min. • Serves: 4

Ingredients

Yam (*jimikand*), peeled, washed	1½ kg
Green chillies, finely chopped	3-4 gm
Ginger (*adrak*), finely chopped	¾ tsp / 10 gm
Salt	1½ tsp / 5 gm
White pepper (*safed mirch*) powder	¾ tsp / 1½ gm
Red chilli powder	¾ tsp / 1½ gm
Chaat masala	¾ tsp / 1½ gm
Green coriander (*hara dhaniya*), finely chopped	¾ tsp / 1 gm
Breadcrumbs	½ cup / 60 gm
Vegetable oil	¾ cup / 170 gm

Method

1. Boil the yam until tender. Drain and when cool enough to handle, grate finely. Squeeze out the excess water.
2. Mix in the other ingredients except oil. Divide the mixture into 8 equal portions. Shape the portions into medallions.
3. Heat the oil in a wok (*kadhai*); shallow fry the medallions, on medium heat, till crisp and golden brown on both sides. Remove with a slotted spoon and drain the excess oil on absorbent kitchen towels.
4. Serve hot.

Cottage cheese and sago kebabs

Prep. time: 1 hr. • Cooking time: 25 min. • Serves: 4

Ingredients

Soft cottage cheese (*chenna*), mashed	500 gm
Sago (*sabut dana*)	100 gm
Spring onions, minced	100 gm
Green chillies, chopped	2-3
Cashew nuts (*kaju*), broken	1/3 cup / 45 gm
Raisins (*kishmish*)	6 tbsp / 60 gm
Cumin (*jeera*) seeds, roasted	1 tsp / 2 gm
Turmeric (*haldi*) powder	1/2 tsp / 1 gm
Garam masala (see p. 8)	1 tsp / 2 gm
Cornflour	3 tbsp / 30 gm
Salt to taste	
Vegetable oil for frying	

Method

1. Cook the soft cottage cheese until it is absolutely dry. When cool, mash again.

2. Boil the sago till soft. Drain and blend to a coarse paste.

3. Mix together all the ingredients and knead. Keep aside for 1/2 hour.

4. Divide the mixture into lemon-sized portions and shape into flat, round cutlets. Heat the oil in a wok (*kadhai*); fry the cutlets, a few at a time, until golden brown. Remove, drain the excess oil and serve hot.

Vegetable seekh kebab

Prep. time: 1 hr. • Cooking time: 10 min. • Serves: 4

Ingredients

Potatoes, boiled	4
Yam (*jimikand*), boiled	500 gm
Cauliflower (*phool gobhi*), cut into florets, boiled .	100 gm
French beans, finely chopped, boiled	100 gm
Carrots (*gajar*), finely chopped, boiled	100 gm
Cottage cheese (*paneer*), mashed	125 gm
Cashew nuts (*kaju*), ground	1/2 cup / 60 gm
Ginger (*adrak*) paste	2 tsp / 12 gm
Garlic (*lasan*) paste	2 tsp / 12 gm
Onions, minced	2/5 cup / 120 gm
Green chillies, minced	2 tsp / 10 gm
Green coriander (*hara dhaniya*), minced	1 cup / 25 gm
Cumin (*jeera*) seeds, roasted	1 tsp / 2 gm
Red chilli powder	1 tsp / 2 gm
Salt to taste	
Vegetable oil for basting	

Method

1. Mash the boiled vegetables together to a fine paste. Add the remaining ingredients (except oil) and knead to a stiff dough. Keep aside for 30 minutes.
2. Spread the mixture along the length of the skewers. Bake in a preheated oven (150-175°C or 300-350°F) for 10 minutes. Remove, baste with oil and bake further for 5 minutes.
3. Remove from the skewers and serve hot.

Green gram pancakes

Prep. time: 3 hrs. • Cooking time: 30 min. • Serves: 2-4

Ingredients

Green gram (moong dal), soaked for 2-3 hours	1¼ cups / 185 gm
Ginger-garlic (adrak-lasan) paste	2 tbsp / 25 gm
Green chillies, chopped	3
Green coriander (hara dhaniya), chopped	1 tbsp / 4 gm
Salt to taste	
Vegetable oil for frying	

Method

1. Drain the green gram and grind to a fine paste, add a little water if required.
2. Add the remaining ingredients (except oil) to the green gram paste and mix well. Add a little more water, if necessary, so that the batter is of dropping consistency.
3. Smear 2 tsp oil in a non-stick pan; pour 2 tbsp of the batter and spread evenly to form a flat, round pancake. Cook on a low flame till both the sides are golden brown. Repeat till all the batter is used up. You can make 6-8 such pancakes.
4. Serve hot with lasan ki chutney (see p. 219).

Semolina fritters

Prep. time: 25 min. • Cooking time: 10 min. • Serves: 4-6

Ingredients

Semolina (*suji*), sieved	1½ cups / 150 gm
Yoghurt (*dahi*)	1 cup / 180 gm
Water	¾ cup / 150 ml
Onions, small, chopped	2
Green chillies, finely chopped	2
Green coriander (*hara dhaniya*), chopped	1 tbsp / 4 gm
Salt to taste	
Asafoetida (*hing*)	a pinch
Vegetable oil for frying	

Method

1. Mix the semolina, yoghurt and water together. Keep aside for 20-30 minutes.
2. Add the onions, green chillies, green coriander, salt, asafoetida and a little oil. Mix well.
3. Heat the oil in a wok (*kadhai*); add spoonfuls of the batter, a few at a time, and deep-fry until crisp and brown. Remove with a slotted spoon and drain the excess oil on absorbent kitchen towels. Repeat till all the batter is used up.
4. Serve hot.

Corn croquettes

Prep. time: 15 min. • Cooking time: 5-10 min. • Serves: 2-3

Ingredients

Corn (*bhutta*), grated	1 cup / 200 gm
Bread, slices	2
Ginger (*adrak*) paste	1 tsp / 6 gm
Green chilli paste	1 tsp / 5 gm
White pepper (*safed mirch*) powder	½ tsp / 1 gm
Green coriander (*hara dhaniya*), chopped	1 tbsp / 4 gm
Salt to taste	
Vegetable oil for frying	

For the mint chutney:

Mint (*pudina*) leaves	1 bunch
Green chillies	2
Onion, small	1
Lemon (*nimbu*) juice	½ tsp / 3 ml
Salt to taste	
Cumin (*jeera*) seeds	1 tsp / 2 gm

Method

1. Mix all the ingredients (except oil and ingredients for the mint chutney) together.
2. Divide the mixture equally into lemon-sized balls. Flatten each piece into the desired shape.
3. Heat the oil in a pan till smoking; shallow fry the croquettes till golden brown. Remove and drain the excess oil on absorbent kitchen towels.
4. **For the mint chutney,** mix and blend all the ingredients to a fine paste.
5. Serve the croquettes hot with this chutney.

Crispy Bengal gram strips

Prep. time: 5 hrs. • Cooking time: 30 min. • Serves: 4-6

Ingredients

Bengal gram (*chana dal*), soaked for 4-5 hours	1¼ cups / 200 gm
Coriander (*dhaniya*) seeds	1 tbsp / 5 gm
Black peppercorns (*sabut kali mirch*)	6-8
Ginger (*adrak*), chopped	2 tsp / 20 gm
Green coriander (*hara dhaniya*), chopped	1 tbsp / 4 gm
Green chillies, chopped	2
Salt to taste	
Red chilli powder	1 tsp / 2 gm
Garam masala (see p. 8)	1 tsp / 2 gm
Vegetable oil for frying	

Method

1. Drain the Bengal gram and then blend with coriander seeds and black peppercorns to a thick paste.
2. Mix the remaining ingredients (except oil) with the paste. Keep aside for 30 minutes.
3. With moist palms, divide and shape the paste into 10 cm flat patties. Heat the oil in a wok (*kadhai*), fry the patties for 2-3 minutes. Remove and drain the excess oil on absorbent towels.
4. When cool, slice the patties into 3-4 strips. Reheat the oil till smoking, lower the heat to medium and fry the strips till crisp and golden brown. Drain the excess oil and serve hot with mint chutney (see p. 214).

Potato baskets

Prep. time: 10-15 min. • Serves: 5-6

Ingredients

Potatoes, large, boiled, peeled	8
For the filling:	
Chickpeas (*kabuli chana*), boiled	³/₄ cup / 115 gm
Chaat masala	1 tbsp / 4 gm
Ginger (*adrak*), finely chopped	1 tbsp / 18 gm
Green chillies, finely chopped	2
Green coriander (*hara dhaniya*), finely chopped	1 tbsp / 4 gm
Lemon (*nimbu*) juice	2 tbsp / 30 ml
Salt to taste	

Method

1. Cut the potatoes in half and carefully scoop out the centres leaving a ½" -shell behind.
2. **For the filling,** mix the chickpeas, *chaat* masala, ginger, green chillies, green coriander, lemon juice and salt together. Press the filling into the potato shells.
3. Serve on a flat dish, hot or cold.

Bharwan Aloo

Vegetable poppadom rolls

Prep. time: 20 min. • Cooking time: 5 min. • Serves: 4

Ingredients

Poppadoms (*pappad*), medium-sized	4
Carrot (*gajar*), medium-sized, chopped	1
Potato, medium-sized, chopped	1
Cauliflower (*phool gobhi*), chopped	100 gm
French beans, chopped	6
Tomatoes, chopped	1
Red chilli powder	½ tsp / 1 gm
Turmeric (*haldi*) powder	½ tsp / 1 gm
Green coriander (*hara dhaniya*), chopped	1 tbsp / 4 gm
Salt to taste	
Vegetable oil for frying	

Method

1. Boil the first four vegetables with a pinch of salt till ¾ done. Drain and keep the vegetables aside to dry.

2. Fry the tomatoes in 1 tbsp oil. Add the boiled vegetables, turmeric powder, red chilli powder and green coriander. Mix well. Remove and keep aside to cool. Divide the mixture equally into 4 portions.

3. Take a poppadom and dip it in water (so that it becomes pliable). Put one portion of this mixture along the centre and roll. Press the ends well to seal. Repeat with the other poppadoms.

4. Heat the oil in a wok (*kadhai*); deep-fry the rolls till crisp. Remove immediately and serve hot.

Grilled cottage cheese rolls

Prep. time: 20 min. • Cooking time: 20 min. • Serves: 4

Ingredients

Cottage cheese (paneer), sliced into 15 × 6 × 0.5 cm pieces	500 gm
For the filling:	
Vegetable oil	5 tbsp / 50 ml
Mushrooms, chopped	150 gm
Capsicum (Shimla mirch), medium-sized, chopped	3-4
Onions, chopped	³/₄ cup / 180 gm
Coconut (nariyal) powder	¹/₂ cup / 100 gm
Cottage cheese (paneer), grated	150 gm
Black cumin (shah jeera) seeds	1 tsp / 2 gm
Cayenne pepper	2 tsp / 4 gm
Dry fenugreek leaves (kasoori methi)	1 tsp / ½ gm
Lemon (nimbu) juice	2 tsp / 10 ml
Salt to taste	
Potatoes, boiled, grated	100 gm
Raisins (kishmish)	¹/₂ cup / 50 gm
Turmeric (haldi) powder	1 tsp / 2 gm
White pepper (safed mirch) powder	4 tsp / 8 gm
For the batter:	
Cornflour	¹/₂ cup / 45 gm
Cream	¹/₂ cup / 100 gm
Gram flour (besan)	¹/₄ cup / 50 gm
Green coriander (hara dhaniya), chopped	4 tsp / 8 gm
Saffron (kesar)	a few strands
Water	4 tsp / 20 ml
For the garnish:	
Chaat masala	a pinch

Carrot (*gajar*), medium-sized, grated |

Lemon (*nimbu*), cut into wedges |

Method

1. **For the filling**, heat the oil in a wok (*kadhai*); sauté the mushrooms, capsicum, onion and coconut powder. Add the cottage cheese and the remaining ingredients for the filling. Stir-fry for a few seconds and then remove from heat.

2. **For the batter**, mix all the ingredients adding just enough water to make a thick paste. Spread the paste on one side of each cottage cheese slice, turn over, spread 3 tsp of the filling and shape into a roll. Similarly, prepare the other rolls.

3. Bake the rolls in a preheated oven at 150-175°C / 300-350°F for 10-12 minutes on low heat.

4. Sprinkle some *chaat* masala over the rolls. Garnish with carrot and lemon wedges.

Fantastic Fenugreek
A teaspoon of ground fenugreek seeds (methi dana) mixed with buttermilk is an effective drink for diarrhoea and dysentry.

Cottage cheese croquettes

Prep. time: 10 min. • Cooking time: 15 min. • Serves: 4

Ingredients

Cottage cheese (*paneer*), grated	500 gm
Green chillies, chopped	4
Green coriander (*hara dhaniya*), chopped	1 tbsp / 4 gm
White pepper (*safed mirch*) powder	1 tsp / 2 gm
Red chilli powder	1 tsp / 2 gm
Carom (*ajwain*) seeds	1/2 tsp / 1 gm
Egg, optional	1
Garam masala (see p. 8)	1 tsp / 2 gm
Gram flour (*besan*)	3/4 cup / 75 gm
Vegetable oil for frying	

Method

1. Mix all the ingredients (except gram flour and oil) in a bowl. Now, add the gram flour and mix for 2 minutes into a smooth paste.
2. Heat the oil in a wok (*kadhai*); shape the mixture into balls and slide them in carefully. Fry till the cottage cheese balls are golden brown and crisp. Remove with a slotted spoon and drain the excess oil on absorbent kitchen towels.
3. Serve hot with mint chutney (see p. 214).

Nepalese split black gram fritters

Prep. time: 10 min. • Cooking time: 15 min. • Serves: 2-4

Ingredients

Split black gram (*urad dal*)	2½ cups / 250 gm
Asafoetida (*hing*)	a pinch
Cumin (*jeera*) powder	½ tsp / 1 gm
Ginger (*adrak*), scraped, ground	1 tsp / 6 gm
Green chillies, ground (optional)	2-3
Salt to taste	
Mustard (*sarson*) seeds	1 tsp / 3 gm
Vegetable oil for frying	

Method

1. Soak the split black gram overnight. Next morning rub between your palms to remove the husk. Grind to a paste.
2. Add all the ingredients and whip with your hands till light and fluffy.
3. Heat the oil till it starts smoking. Reduce heat and drop a teaspoonful of the mixture. Fry till brown. Remove with a slotted spoon and drain on absorbent kitchen towels. Repeat till all the mixture is used up.
4. Serve hot.

Morel mushroom cutlets

Prep. time: 25 min. • Cooking time: 30 min. • Serves: 4

Ingredients

Morel mushrooms (*guchhi*), chopped	150 gm
Potatoes, boiled, peeled	3
Green peas (*mattar*), boiled	50 gm
Onions, medium-sized, finely chopped	3
Green chillies, finely chopped	3
Ginger (*adrak*), finely chopped	1 tsp / 10 gm
Coconut (*nariyal*), grated	1 tbsp / 4 gm
Red chilli powder	1 tsp / 2 gm
Turmeric (*haldi*) powder	½ tsp / 1 gm
Green coriander (*hara dhaniya*), chopped	1 tbsp / 4 gm
Breadcrumbs	2 tbsp / 30 gm
Gram flour (*besan*)	1 cup / 100 gm
Salt	a pinch

Method

1. Mix the first eleven ingredients together in a bowl, adding the breadcrumbs last.
2. In a large bowl, make a thick, smooth batter with gram flour, salt and a little water.
3. Divide and shape the mushroom mixture into flat, round lemon-sized cutlets.
4. Heat the oil in a frying pan till smoking; dip each cutlet in the gram flour batter and fry till evenly crisp and golden brown. Remove and drain on absorbent kitchen towels.
5. Serve hot with mint chutney (see p. 214).

Bengali aubergine fritters

Prep. time: 15 min. • Cooking time: 10 min. • Serves: 2-4

Ingredients

Aubergines (*baingan*), large, cut into half rounds	4
For the batter:	
Gram flour (*besan*)	I cup / 100 gm
Water	5 tbsp / 75 ml
Refined flour (*maida*)	1/4 cup / 25 gm
Onion seeds (*kalonji*)	I tsp / 2 gm
Red chilli powder	1/2 tsp / I gm
Baking soda	1/2 tsp / 3 gm

Ghee / Vegetable oil for frying

Method

1. **For the batter,** mix the gram flour, water, refined flour, onion seeds, red chilli powder and baking soda together. Keep aside for at least 2 hours.
2. Heat the ghee / oil in a wok (*kadhai*); lower the flame. Dip the aubergine pieces in the batter and then fry in the hot oil till they are tender and golden brown. Remove with a slotted spoon and drain the excess oil on absorbent kitchen towels.
3. Serve immediately.

Kashmiri lotus stem fingers

Nadur Mónji

Prep. time: 15 min. • Cooking time: 15 min. • Serves: 6-8

Ingrèdients

Lotus stems (*kamal kakri*)	500 gm
Refined flour (*maida*)	1/2 cup / 50 gm
Bicarbonate of soda	a pinch
Red chilli powder	1 tsp / 2 gm
Salt to taste	
Water	1/2 cup / 100 ml
Red colour (optional)	3-4 drops
Vegetable oil for frying	

Method

1. Scrape the lotus stems and cut off the ends. Wash thoroughly under running water, ensuring that no mud remains in the stems.

2. Cut the stems into 3" pieces and then slice each piece into 4-6 fingers. Wash well again.

3. In a big bowl, mix the refined flour, bicarbonate of soda, red chilli powder, salt and enough water to make a batter of dropping consistency. Add the red colour.

4. Heat the oil in a deep pan; dip each lotus stem piece into the batter and then deep-fry until golden. Remove with a slotted spoon and drain the excess oil on absorbent kitchen towels.

5. Serve hot.

Prep. time: 2 hrs.   •   Cooking time: 15 min.   •   Serves: 2-4

Ingredients

Poppy seeds (*khuskhus*)	300 gm
Potatoes, boiled, mashed	100 gm
Gram flour (*besan*)	¼ cup / 25 gm
Green chillies	3-4
Onions, chopped	2 tbsp / 25 gm
Salt to taste	
Vegetable oil	½ cup / 85 ml

Method

1. Soak the poppy seeds in double the quantity of water for 2 hours and keep aside. Grind to a paste.
2. Mix the potatoes with the gram flour, green chillies and onions. Add the salt and poppy seed paste. Mix well.
3. Divide the mixture equally into 4 balls. Flatten the balls and keep aside.
4. Heat the oil in a pan; shallow fry the balls till golden brown. Remove with a slotted spoon and drain the excess oil on absorbent kitchen towels.
5. Serve hot with *sonth* (see p. 228).

Bengali flour crispies

Prep. time: 15 min. • Cooking time: 10 min. • Serves: 2-4

Ingredients

Refined flour (*maida*)	2½ cups / 250 gm
Ghee	2 tbsp / 30 gm
Salt	2 tsp / 8 gm
Water	⅓ cup / 60 ml
Onion seeds (*kalonji*)	4 tsp / 6 gm
Vegetable oil for deep-frying	

Method

1. Mix the refined flour, ghee and salt together. Add the onion seeds and water. Knead into a firm dough.
2. Divide the dough into small equal-sized balls.
3. Flatten the balls and roll them out into discs. Dust flour on both sides of the discs and then fold each into quarters (will be triangular in shape).
4. Heat the oil in a wok (*kadhai*); fry the quarters, over a medium flame, till crisp and golden. Remove with a slotted spoon and drain the excess oil on absorbent kitchen towels.
5. Store in airtight containers. These last up to 2-3 weeks.

Prep. time: 15 min. • Serves: 2-4

Ingredients

Puffed rice (*murmura*)	250 gm
Onion, finely chopped	2 tbsp / 25 gm
Potato, boiled, peeled, finely chopped	30 gm
Tomato, finely chopped	30 gm
Cucumber, finely chopped	½
Ginger (*adrak*), finely chopped	2 tsp / 12 gm
Green chillies, finely chopped	4-5
Peanuts (*moongphalli*), fried	2 tbsp / 30 gm
Sprouted black gram (*kala chana*), soaked, drained	2 tsp / 10 gm
Mustard (*sarson*) oil	4 tsp / 8 ml
Salt	1 tsp / 4 gm

Method

1. Combine all the ingredients except the mustard oil and salt in a bowl. Mix gently with a fork.
2. Now add the mustard oil and salt. Mix gently again.
3. Serve as a snack at teatime.

Bengali Jhal Muri

Fried pressed rice

Prep. time: 30 min. • Cooking time: 10 min. • Serves: 2-4

Ingredients

Pressed rice (*chidwa*)	4 cups / 200 gm
Vegetable oil for frying	
Peanuts (*moongphalli*)	¼ cup / 50 gm
Potatoes, julienned	50 gm
Salt	1 tsp / 4 gm
Black peppercorns (*sabut kali mirch*), crushed	1 tsp / 2 gm

Method

1. Heat the oil in a wok (*kadhai*); fry the pressed rice, peanuts and potatoes separately. Remove with a slotted spoon and drain the excess oil on absorbent kitchen towels.
2. In a big bowl, combine all the ingredients.
3. Add salt and black pepper powder; mix gently till the whole mixture is seasoned.
4. This can be served hot or at room temperature.

Steamed rice flour cakes

Prep. time: 7½ hrs. • Cooking time: 10-15 min. • Serves: 4

Ingredients

Parboiled rice	1¾ cups / 350 gm
Split black gram (*urad dal*), soaked for 1 hour	1½ cups / 150 gm
Salt to taste	

Method

1. Blend the parboiled rice to a coarse paste and soak in water for 10 minutes.
2. Drain and blend the black gram to a fluffy paste.
3. Drain the excess water from the rice paste and mix with the black gram paste. Add salt and keep the mixture aside to ferment for 6 hours in a warm place.
4. Grease the *idli* moulds with groundnut oil and pour equal quantities of the rice mixture into each moulds.
5. Steam in a steamer or a pressure cooker for 8-10 minutes.
6. Remove the *idli* from the *idli* moulds and serve hot with *sambhar* (see p. 161) and coconut chutney (see p. 215).

Vegetable rice pancakes

Uttapam

Prep. time: 1½ hrs. • Cooking time: 10-15 min. • Serves: 4

Ingredients

Rice, Basmati, soaked for 1 hour	1¼ cups / 225 gm
Split black gram (*urad dal*), soaked for 1 hour	1 cup / 100 gm
Yoghurt (*dahi*)	3 tbsp / 90 gm
Bicarbonate of soda	1 tsp / 6 gm
Onion, chopped	1
Green chillies, chopped	4
Coconut (*nariyal*), grated	5 tbsp / 20 gm
Green coriander (*hara dhaniya*), chopped	5 tbsp / 20 gm
Vegetable oil	½ cup / 85 ml

Method

1. Drain and blend the rice and black gram. Keep aside.
2. Beat the yoghurt and bicarbonate of soda into the rice mixture till light and frothy.
3. Add the onion, green chillies, coconut and green coriander, mix well. Keep aside for 20 minutes.
4. Heat a griddle (*tawa*) or a hot plate and brush with oil. Spread a ladleful of the rice batter and cook on both sides until crisp and golden brown.
5. Remove, drain the excess oil on absorbent kitchen towels and serve hot with *sambhar* (see p. 161) and coconut chutney (see p. 215).

Tandoori and Dry

Stuffed bitter gourd

Prep. time: 30 min. • Cooking time: 45 min. • Serves: 4

Ingredients

Bitter gourd (*karela*)	1 kg
Mustard oil for frying	
For the filling:	
Ghee	4 tbsp / 60 gm
Asafoetida (*hing*) powder	a pinch
Sugar	2 tsp / 6 gm
Salt	2 tsp / 8 gm
Potatoes, cut into ½" cubes	120 gm
Cumin (*jeera*) seeds	½ tsp / 1 gm
Lentil (*masoor dal*), washed, drained	4 tbsp / 80 gm
Tamarind (*imli*) pulp	2 tsp / 10 gm
Fennel (*saunf*) seeds	2 tsp / 3 gm
Red chilli powder	1 tsp / 2 gm
Onion paste	3 tbsp / 75 gm
Garlic (*lasan*) paste	2 tsp / 12 gm
Ginger (*adrak*), chopped	½ tbsp / 10 gm
Green chillies, chopped	2-3
Green coriander (*hara dhaniya*), chopped	2 tsp / 5 gm
Water	½ cup / 100 ml
Mustard oil	3 tbsp / 30 ml
Yoghurt (*dahi*)	⅓ cup / 60 gm
Salt to taste	
Red chilli powder	1 tsp / 2 gm
Ginger (*adrak*) paste	1½ tsp / 9 gm

Method

1. Scrape the bitter gourd and boil till half cooked. When cool, slit and remove the seeds. Squeeze out the excess water, gently.
2. Heat the mustard oil in a wok (*kadhai*); deep-fry the bitter gourd till crisp. Remove with a slotted spoon and drain the excess oil on absorbent kitchen towels. Keep aside.
3. **For the filling,** heat the ghee in a pan; add asafoetida and all the other ingredients. Stir-fry for a few minutes. Then pour in the water and cook till the water is absorbed. Remove from the fire.
4. When cool, stuff the bitter gourd with this mixture and secure by wrapping a thread around, several times.
5. In a separate pan, heat the mustard oil; add the stuffed bitter gourd and the remaining ingredients. Cook till the mixture is dry. Remove and serve hot.

Stuffed courgettes

Prep. time: 10 min. • Cooking time: 25 min. • Serves: 2-4

Ingredients

Courgettes (*teenda*), washed, dried	4
Vegetable oil for frying	
Onion, finely chopped	1
Tomatoes, chopped	2
Garam masala (see p. 8)	1 tbsp / 4 gm
Red chilli powder	1 tsp / 2 gm
Mango powder (*amchur*)	2 tsp / 4 gm
Salt to taste	
Cream	4 tbsp / 80 gm

Method

1. Slice the top of the courgettes to form a lid. Scoop out the centre and keep aside.

2. Heat the oil in a pan; deep-fry the courgettes for 1-2 minutes. Remove with a slotted spoon and drain the excess oil on absorbent kitchen towels. Keep aside.

3. Heat 4 tbsp oil in a pan; sauté the onion until transparent. Mix in the tomatoes and cook for 4-5 minutes. Add the garam masala, red chilli powder, mango powder, salt and cream. Cook covered on low heat for a few minutes.

4. Fill each courgette cup with this mixture, replace the lid, place them on a baking tray and bake in a preheated oven (175°C or 350°F) for 5-7 minutes. Remove the lid and serve hot.

Dum Aloo

Prep. time: 20 min. • Cooking time: 20 min. • Serves: 4

Ingredients

Potatoes, small, boiled, peeled	20-25
Potatoes, boiled, peeled, grated	200 gm
Ghee	1 tbsp / 15 gm
Onions, grated	5⅓ tbsp / 66 gm
Ginger (adrak) paste	2 tbsp / 36 gm
Garlic (lasan) paste	2 tbsp / 36 gm
Red chilli powder	2 tsp / 4 gm
Turmeric (haldi) powder	1 tsp / 2 gm
Garam masala (see p. 8)	2 tsp / 4 gm
Lemon (nimbu) juice	1 tbsp / 15 ml
Salt to taste	
Vegetable oil	3½ tbsp / 35 gm
Bay leaf (tej patta)	1
Cinnamon (dalchini), 1" sticks	2
Cloves (laung)	6
Green cardamoms (choti elaichi)	6
Black cumin (shah jeera) seeds	1 tsp / 2 gm
Yoghurt (dahi), whisked	¾ cup / 135 gm

Method

1. Heat the ghee in a pan. Add half the grated onion, ginger and garlic pastes and fry for 4-5 minutes. Add the grated potatoes, 1 tsp red chilli powder, ½ tsp turmeric powder and 1 tsp garam masala. Season with ½ tbsp lemon juice and salt. Keep the filling aside.

2. Scoop the small potatoes from the centre. Fry these

potatoes carefully. When cool, stuff each potato with the potato filling. Keep aside, covered.

3. Heat the oil in a pan over medium heat; add the bay leaf, cinnamon sticks, cloves, green cardamoms, black cumin seeds and fry for 30-50 seconds or until they begin to crackle.

4. Add the remaining grated onions, ginger and garlic pastes and fry for 2-3 minutes. Add the remaining turmeric powder and red chilli powder and fry over medium heat for 5-6 minutes.

5. Stir in the yoghurt and cook till the mixture is absolutely dry. Add the remaining garam masala. Season with salt.

6. Arrange the stuffed potatoes carefully in the pan. Add the remaining lemon juice. Cover the pan and cook for 3-4 minutes on very low heat.

Curable Cumin

Dry cough can be cured by sipping a mixture of ghee and cumin (jeera) powder.

Spicy potato delicacy

Prep. time: 30 min. • Cooking time: 45 min. • Serves: 4

Ingredients

Potatoes, diced into 1/2" cubes	600 gm
For the paste:	
Green chillies	2
Roasted gram (*chana*)	2 tbsp / 20 gm
Cumin (*jeera*) seeds	1 tsp / 2 gm
Black peppercorns (*sabut kali mirch*)	9-10
Ginger (*adrak*), chopped	1 tsp / 10 gm
Cinnamon (*dalchini*), 1" stick	1
Cloves (*laung*)	2
Coconut (*nariyal*), grated	2 tbsp / 8 gm
Vegetable oil	3 tbsp / 30 ml
Asafoetida (*hing*)	a pinch
Mustard (*sarson*) seeds	1 tsp / 2 gm
Dry red chillies (*sookhi lal mirch*)	2
Curry leaves (*kadhi patta*)	6
Onions, chopped	2 tbsp / 25 gm
Turmeric (*haldi*) powder	1 tsp / 2 gm
Tomatoes, chopped	2 tbsp / 30 gm
Salt to taste	
Green coriander (*hara dhaniya*), chopped	1 tsp / 2 gm

Method

1. **For the paste,** mix all the ingredients in a blender with a little water. Keep aside.
2. Heat the oil in a wok (*kadhai*); add the asafoetida,

mustard seeds, dry red chillies and curry leaves. When the mustard seeds start spluttering, add the onions and sauté lightly.

3. Add the turmeric powder and the tomatoes. Stir-fry for 2-3 minutes.

4. Now add the potatoes, salt and sufficient water to cover the potatoes. Cover and simmer till the potatoes are tender.

5. Add the prepared paste. Mix and simmer gently for 4-5 minutes or till the mixture is dry.

6. Serve hot garnished with green coriander.

Note: Saagu can be made with mixed vegetables also.

Tasty Leftovers

*Leftover pulses and vegetables
make excellent stuffed parathas.
They are highly nutritious too.*

Spicy potato with fresh mint and coriander

Prep. time: 20 min. • Cooking time: 30 min. • Serves: 3-4

Ingredients

Potatoes, peeled, diced	600 gm
Mint (*pudina*) leaves, fresh	1 tsp / 2 gm
Lemon (*nimbu*) juice	2 tbsp / 30 ml
Green chillies	3
Green coriander (*hara dhaniya*), chopped	½ cup / 12 gm
Vegetable oil	½ cup / 85 ml
Ginger (*adrak*) paste	2 tsp / 12 gm
Garlic (*lasan*) paste	2 tsp / 12 gm
Cumin (*jeera*) powder	1 tsp / 1½ gm
Coriander (*dhaniya*) powder	1½ tsp / 2 gm
Red chilli paste	1½ tsp / 7 gm
Salt to taste	
Water	1¼ cups / 250 ml

Method

1. Blend the mint leaves, lemon juice, green chillies and green coriander into a fine paste.

2. Heat the oil in a heavy-bottomed pan; add the ginger-garlic pastes and potatoes. Stir-fry for 2-3 minutes. Add the cumin powder, coriander powder and the red chilli paste. Mix well. Add salt and water. Bring the mixture to the boil and simmer till the potatoes are cooked.

3. Add the green paste and stir-fry for 4-5 minutes till the mixture is dry.

4. Serve hot.

Potatoes flavoured with pomegranate seeds

Prep. time: 30 min. • Cooking time: 15-20 min. • Serves: 4

Ingredients

Potatoes, boiled, cut into 1½" cubes	1 kg
Pomegranate seeds (*anardana*), dried, crushed	1 cup
Butter	½ cup / 85 gm
Coriander (*dhaniya*) powder	1 tbsp / 6 gm
Turmeric (*haldi*) powder	½ tsp / 1 gm
Red chilli powder	1 tsp / 2 gm
Salt to taste	
Green chillies, slit	6
Green coriander (*hara dhaniya*), chopped	1 tbsp / 8 gm

Method

1. Heat the butter in a heavy-bottomed pan; add the coriander powder, turmeric powder, red chilli powder and half of the pomegranate seeds. Mix thoroughly.

2. Add the potatoes, salt and green chillies. Mix gently, so that the spices coat the potatoes evenly. Reduce the heat to low and simmer for 10-15 minutes. Remove the pan from the heat.

3. Serve hot garnished with green coriander and the remaining pomegranate seeds.

Spicy potato delight

Prep. time: 20 min. • Cooking time: 30 min. • Serves: 4

Ingredients

Potatoes, medium-sized, peeled	8
Vegetable oil for frying	
For the filling:	
Black cumin (*shah jeera*) seeds	2 tsp / 5 gm
Aniseed (*moti saunf*)	3 tsp / 4½ gm
Onions, chopped	2
Black cardamom (*badi elaichi*) seeds, pounded	2 tsp / 4 gm
Raisins (*kishmish*)	7 tbsp / 70 gm
Cashew nuts (*kaju*)	5 tbsp / 75 gm
Salt to taste	
Vegetable oil	½ cup / 85 ml
Onions, sliced, brown	½ cup / 120 gm
Mace (*javitri*)	1 tsp / 2 gm
Black cumin (*shah jeera*) seeds	1 tsp / 2 gm
Black cardamoms (*badi elaichi*)	4
Cloves (*laung*)	6
Aniseed (*moti saunf*)	3 tsp / 5 gm
Ginger (*adrak*) paste	1½ tsp / 9 gm
Garlic (*lasan*) paste	1½ tsp / 9 gm
Cumin (*jeera*) powder	2 tsp / 3 gm
Coriander (*dhaniya*) powder	3 tsp / 5 gm
Salt to taste	
Almond (*badam*) paste	40 gm
Red chilli paste	3 tsp / 15 gm
Yoghurt (*dahi*)	1¼ cups / 225 gm
Tomato purée	1 cup / 200 gm

Method

1. With a sharp knife, carefully scoop out the inside portion of the potatoes. Keep them aside and fry the potato shells to a golden brown. Keep aside.

2. **For the filling**, in the same oil, sauté the black cumin seeds and aniseed. Add the onions and sauté till transparent. Add the scooped out portion of the potatoes, black cardamom powder, raisins and cashew nuts. Stir-fry for a few minutes. Season with salt. Keep aside to cool.

3. When cool enough to handle, stuff the potato shells with the prepared filling.

4. Heat the oil in a thick-bottomed pan; add the onions, whole spices, ginger-garlic pastes and all the powdered spices. Mix well.

5. Add the rest of the ingredients and fry for 6-8 minutes.

6. Carefully place the stuffed potatoes in the mixture. Cover the pan and cook in *dum* for 10 minutes. Remove the potatoes and place them on a serving dish.

7. Strain the thick gravy and pour over the potatoes. Serve hot.

A spicy potato preparation

Prep. time: 10 min. • Cooking time: 30 min. • Serves: 4

Ingredients

Potatoes, boiled, cubed	900 gm
Vegetable oil	5 tbsp / 50 ml
Dry red chillies (*sookhi lal mirch*), cut into half	5
Mustard seeds (*rai*)	1 tsp / 3 gm
Onions, chopped	½ cup / 120 gm
Garlic (*lasan*), chopped	4 tsp / 12 gm
Ginger (*adrak*), chopped	4 tsp / 40 gm
Red chilli powder	2 tsp / 4 gm
Turmeric (*haldi*) powder	1 tsp / 2 gm
Coriander (*dhaniya*) powder	2 tsp / 3 gm
Salt to taste	
Tomatoes, skinned, chopped	300 gm
Green chillies, chopped	3
Lemon (*nimbu*) juice	1 tbsp / 15 ml
Butter	4 tsp / 20 gm

Method

1. Heat the oil in a pan; add the dry red chillies and mustard seeds. Sauté over medium heat until they begin to crackle.
2. Add the onions, garlic, ginger and sauté over high heat for 5-6 minutes. Add the red chilli powder, turmeric powder, coriander powder and salt. Stir well.
3. Add the tomatoes and simmer on low heat until the oil separates from the gravy. Add the potatoes, green chillies, lemon juice and butter. Cook for 5 minutes. Remove from heat and serve.

Delicately spiced fried potatoes

Prep. time: 20 min. ● Cooking time: 25 min. ● Serves: 2-4

Ingredients

Potatoes, long, peeled, chopped into 6"-long pieces, soaked in water	500 gm
Mustard (*sarson*) oil	1 cup / 170 ml
Fenugreek seeds (*methi dana*)	1/2 tsp / 1 1/2 gm
Turmeric (*haldi*) powder	1/2 tsp / 1 gm
Salt to taste	
Grind to a paste:	
Garlic (*lasan*) cloves	8
Ginger (*adrak*)	1 tbsp / 24 gm
Green chillies	4-5
Black peppercorns (*sabut kali mirch*)	1 tsp / 5 gm

Method

1. Heat the mustard oil in a pan; add the fenugreek seeds. When it begins to crackle, add the drained potatoes and turmeric powder. Stir well.

2. Add salt and cook on a high flame stirring once or twice. Avoid breaking the potatoes. Once the outer coat of the potatoes are firm and evenly coloured to light brown, drain the excess oil, if any.

3. Add the ground paste, cook over a low flame for 4-5 minutes, stirring occasionally. The paste does not have to be brown, only cooked. By this time the potatoes too will be reddish. Serve hot.

Mustard-flavoured mashed potatoes

Prep. time: 20 min. • Cooking time: 5 min. • Serves: 2-4

Ingredients

Potatoes, whole, boiled, peeled	300 gm
Salt to taste	
Green chillies, chopped	2-3
Mustard (*sarson*) oil	1 tbsp / 10 ml

Method

1. Mash the potatoes; add salt, green chillies and mustard oil.
2. Shape the potato mixture into small balls.
3. Serve with steamed rice.

Turmeric Magic

To prevent the pressure cooker from turning black after boiling potatoes, add a little turmeric powder.

Potato with black pepper

Prep. time: 20 min. ● Cooking time: 5 min. ● Serves: 2-4

Ingredients

Potatoes, boiled, diced	300 gm
Ghee	2 tbsp / 30 gm
Black peppercorns (*sabut kali mirch*), crushed	4 tsp / 8 gm
Salt to taste	

Method

1. Heat the ghee in a wok (*kadhai*); add the potatoes and fry for 2 minutes.
2. Add the black pepper and salt. Toss till the potatoes are coated well with the mixture.
3. Serve hot.

Crispy Treat
Do not discard the potato peels.
Wash them, apply salt and fry till
crisp. Sprinkle a little chaat masala
and serve. It makes a delicious snack.

Mixed vegetables with poppy seeds

Prep. time: 1 hr. • Cooking time: 30 min. • Serves: 2-4

Ingredients

Poppy seeds (*khuskhus*), soaked in ½ cup water	50 gm
Green chillies	3
Broad beans, cut into fingers	50 gm
Cauliflower (*phool gobhi*), cut into small florets	50 gm
Aubergines (*baingan*), cut into fingers	60 gm
Radish (*mooli*), cut into fingers	30 gm
Cabbage (*bandh gobhi*), chopped	60 gm
Vegetable oil	3 tbsp / 30 ml
Turmeric (*haldi*) powder	2 tsp / 4 gm
Onion seeds (*kalonji*)	1 tsp / 2 gm
Dry red chillies (*sookhi lal mirch*)	3
Water	¼ cup / 50 ml
Salt to taste	

Method

1. Drain the poppy seeds and grind to a paste with green chillies. Keep aside.
2. Heat the oil in a wok (*kadhai*); add the turmeric powder, onion seeds and dry red chillies, sauté for half a minute.
3. Add all the vegetables and sauté for about 4 minutes. Add the water, poppy seed paste and salt. Cook till the water is absorbed and the vegetables are cooked.
4. Serve hot.

Bengali potato delight

Prep. time: 15 min. • Cooking time: 30 min. • Serves: 2-4

Ingredients

Potatoes, thinly sliced	200 gm
Onions, thinly sliced	½ cup / 120 gm
Vegetable oil	2 tbsp / 20 gm
Turmeric (*haldi*) powder	1 tsp / 2 gm
Salt to taste	
Red chilli powder	2 tsp / 4 gm
Water	½ cup / 100 ml

Method

1. Heat the oil in a wok (*kadhai*); add the onions and sauté till transparent.
2. Add the potatoes and sauté for 3-4 minutes. Add the turmeric powder, salt, red chilli powder and water.
3. Cook over a medium flame till the potatoes are done and the mixture is dry.
4. Serve hot.

Cottage cheese with onions

Prep. time: 10 min. • Cooking time: 10 min. • Serves: 4

Ingredients

Cottage cheese (*paneer*), cut into ½" cubes	900 gm
Button onions	300 gm
Vegetable oil	4 tbsp / 40 ml
Green cardamoms (*choti elaichi*)	3
Cumin (*jeera*) seeds	½ tsp / 1 gm
Turmeric (*haldi*) powder	1½ tsp / 3 gm
Red chilli powder	1 tsp / 2 gm
Capsicum (*Shimla mirch*), cut into squares	120 gm
Tomatoes, cut into ½" cubes	150 gm
Garam masala (see p. 8)	3 tsp / 6 gm
Salt to taste	
Green coriander (*hara dhaniya*), chopped	3 tsp / 6 gm
Lemon (*nimbu*) juice	2 tsp / 10 ml

Method

1. Heat the oil in a pan; add the green cardamoms and cumin seeds and sauté over medium heat until they begin to crackle. Add the turmeric powder and red chilli powder and sauté for 30 seconds.

2. Add the capsicum, button onions and tomatoes; stir-fry for another 30 seconds over high heat. Now add the cottage cheese, garam masala and salt. Mix for 30 seconds. Cook covered for 6 minutes.

3. Serve hot garnished with green coriander and sprinkled with lemon juice.

Stir-fried spinach with cottage cheese

Prep. time: 25 min. • Cooking time: 30 min. • Serves: 4

Ingredients

Spinach (*palak*)	1 kg
Cottage cheese (*paneer*), cubed	400 gm
Vegetable oil	4 tbsp / 40 ml
Cumin (*jeera*) seeds	1 tsp / 2 gm
Garlic (*lasan*) cloves	10 gm
Dry red chillies (*sookhi lal mirch*)	2
Coriander (*dhaniya*) powder	½ tsp / 1¾ gm
Cumin (*jeera*) powder	½ tsp / 1¾ gm
Red chilli powder	½ tsp / 1 gm
Salt to taste	

Method

1. Blanch the spinach and drain. When cool, chop coarsely.
2. Heat the oil in a wok (*kadhai*); add the cumin seeds, garlic and sauté until the garlic changes colour. Add the dry red chillies and stir for ½ a minute. Add the spinach, coriander powder, cumin powder and red chilli powder. Mix well.
3. Add the cottage cheese and stir-fry for 5 minutes. Season with salt.
4. Serve hot.

Stir-fried spinach with tomato

Prep. time: 10 min. • Cooking time: 15 min. • Serves: 4

Ingredients

Spinach (*palak*), fresh or frozen, washed, roughly chopped	1 kg
Tomatoes, chopped	250 gm
Vegetable oil	4 tbsp / 40 ml
Dry red chillies (*sookhi lal mirch*), cut in half	8
Cumin (*jeera*) seeds	1 tsp / 2 gm
Onions, sliced or chopped	½ cup / 120 gm
Garlic (*lasan*), peeled, cut lengthwise	4 tbsp / 50 gm
Red chilli powder	1 tsp / 2 gm
Turmeric (*haldi*) powder	1 tsp / 2 gm
Asafoetida (*hing*) powder	a pinch
Salt to taste	
Ginger (*adrak*), julienned	2 tsp / 6 gm

Method

1. Heat the oil in a wok (*kadhai*); reduce heat, add the dry red chillies, cumin seeds, onions, garlic, red chilli powder, turmeric powder and asafoetida. Stir-fry for 2-3 minutes.
2. Add the tomatoes and cook for 2 minutes. Add the spinach and stir-fry. Sprinkle salt and cook covered over low heat for 6-7 minutes.
3. Serve hot garnished with ginger.

Spinach and potato delight

Prep. time: 25 min. ● Cooking time: 25 min. ● Serves: 4

Ingredients

Spinach (*palak*), finely chopped	I kg
Potatoes, boiled, cubed	250 gm
Water	10 cups / 2 lt
Salt to taste	
Maize flour (*makkai ka atta*)	2 tsp / 10 gm
Ghee	2 tbsp / 20 gm
Onions, chopped	5 tsp / 30 gm
Ginger (*adrak*), finely chopped	5 tsp / 30 gm
Green chillies, finely chopped	3
Cream	2 tsp / 12 gm

Method

1. Boil the spinach in salted water for 10 minutes, drain the excess water. When slightly cool, blend the boiled spinach in a blender.
2. Reheat the spinach purée, add the potatoes and mix well.
3. Add the maize flour gradually, and cook for 10 minutes.
4. Heat the ghee in a separate pan; add the onions and half the ginger, sauté till brown. Add the green chillies and sauté for 1 minute.
5. Pour this over the potato-spinach mixture, stir well and bring the mixture to the boil.
6. Serve hot garnished with the remaining ginger and cream.

Stir-fried spinach

Prep. time: 10 min. • Cooking time: 15 min. • Serves: 4-5

Ingredients

Spinach (*palak*), roughly chopped	I kg
Vegetable oil	4 tbsp / 40 ml
Dry red chillies (*sookhi lal mirch*), cut in half	8
Onions, sliced or chopped	½ cup / 120 gm
Garlic (*lasan*), peeled, cut lengthwise	4 tbsp / 50 gm
Red chilli powder	I tsp / 2 gm
Turmeric (*haldi*) powder	I tsp / 2 gm
Asafoetida (*hing*)	a pinch
Salt to taste	

Method

1. Heat the oil in a wok (*kadhai*) to smoking point. Reduce heat, add the dry red chillies, onions, garlic, red chilli powder, turmeric powder and asafoetida and stir-fry for 2-3 minutes.
2. Immediately add the spinach and stir-fry.
3. Add salt, cover and cook on very low heat for 6-7 minutes.
4. Serve hot.

Sun-dried dumplings with spinach

Prep. time: 15 min. • Cooking time: 15 min. • Serves: 2-4

Ingredients

Spinach (*palak*), chopped	250 gm
Sun-dried dumplings (*wadi**)	10 gm
Vegetable oil	2 tbsp / 20 ml
Bay leaves (*tej patta*)	2
Turmeric (*haldi*) powder	1 tsp / 1 gm
Water	¼ cup / 50 ml
Salt to taste	
Sugar	2 tsp / 6 gm

Method

1. Heat the oil in a wok (*kadhai*); fry the sun-dried dumplings and keep aside.
2. In the same oil, add the bay leaves, turmeric powder and spinach. Fry for 2 minutes.
3. Add the water, sun-dried dumplings, salt and sugar. Cook till the water is absorbed and the spinach is tender
4. Serve hot.

*Wadi: Small, sun-dried dumplings made with black gram. The black gram is soaked, ground to a paste and mixed with spices. Small dumplings of the paste are then spread on plastic sheets and left in the sun to dry and become hard. These are also easily available at all convenience stores.

Lightly spiced Nepalese spinach

Prep. time: 10 min. ● Cooking time: 10 min. ● Serves: 2-4

Ingredients

Spinach (*palak*), washed, drained	500 gm
Mustard (*sarson*) oil	2 tbsp / 20 ml
Carom seeds (*ajwain*)	1 tsp / 1½ gm
Dry red chillies (*sookhi lal mirch*), halved	2-3
Salt to taste	

Method

1. Heat the oil, preferably in an iron pan. When smoking hot, lower the flame and add the carom seeds and dry red chillies.
2. Add the spinach and salt, toss well. Cook for 4-5 minutes.
3. Remove the pan from the heat and serve.

Instant Relief

If you burn your fingers while holding a hot vessel, just apply some flouride toothpaste.

Stir-fried morel mushrooms

Prep. time: 10 min. • Cooking time: 15 min. • Serves: 4-5

Ingredients

Morel mushrooms (*guchhi*), quartered	600 gm
Vegetable oil	²/₃ cup / 115 ml
Cabbage (*bandh gobhi*), shredded	100 gm
Dry red chillies (*sookhi lal mirch*), pounded	4
Coriander (*dhaniya*) seeds, pounded	1 tsp / 2 gm
Onions, sliced	¹/₃ cup / 80 gm
Garlic (*lasan*) paste	4 tsp / 24 gm
Garam masala (see p. 8)	2 tsp / 4 gm
Salt to taste	
Tomatoes, chopped	500 gm
Green chillies, chopped	4
Ginger (*adrak*), chopped	6 tsp / 40 gm
Green coriander (*hara dhaniya*), chopped	4 tsp / 8 gm
Capsicum (*Shimla mirch*), julienned	60 gm

Method

1. Heat 2 tbsp oil in a pan; sauté the morel mushrooms and cabbage separately till soft. Keep aside.

2. Heat the remaining oil; sauté the onions till transparent. Add the garlic paste, dry red chillies, coriander seeds, garam masala and salt. Stir for 30 seconds. Add the tomatoes and cook till the oil separates. Add the green chillies, ginger, 2 tsp green coriander, morel mushrooms and cabbage. Cook for a few minutes. Garnish with capsicum and the remaining green coriander. Serve hot.

Morel Mushrooms with peas and spring onions

Prep. time: 30 min. • Cooking time: 30 min. • Serves: 4

Ingredients

Morel mushrooms (*guchhi*), quartered	800 gm
Green peas (*mattar*), shelled, boiled	120 gm
Spring onions (*hara pyaz*), finely chopped	120 gm
Vegetable oil	$^1/_3$ cup / 55 ml
Garlic (*lasan*), chopped	2 tbsp / 25 gm
Onions, sliced	$^1/_2$ cup / 120 gm
Salt to taste	
Red chilli powder	$^1/_2$ tsp / 1 gm
Tomato purée	1 cup / 200 gm
Water	1 cup / 200 ml
Garam masala (see p. 8)	1 tsp / 2 gm
Almond (*badam*) paste	2 tbsp / 30 gm

Method

1. Heat the oil in a saucepan; add the garlic and sauté till brown. Add the onions and sauté till golden brown. Add salt, red chilli powder, tomato purée and water, cook for a minute. Remove from heat, and strain the gravy into another saucepan.

2. Reheat the strained gravy and cook till almost all the liquid has evaporated and the mixture is sizzling. Add the morel mushrooms and spring onions and cook for 5 minutes. Add the peas and garam masala, simmer till the mushrooms are done. Stir in the almond paste and cook till the gravy reaches a sauce-like consistency.

Morel mushrooms in a hot tomato sauce

Prep. time: 15 min. • Cooking time: 20 min. • Serves: 4

Ingredients

Morel mushrooms (*gucchi*), washed, halved	800 gm
Vegetable oil	4 tbsp / 40 ml
Dry red chillies (*sookhi lal mirch*)	10
Onions, chopped	½ cup / 120 gm
Ginger (*adrak*) paste	6 tsp / 35 gm
Garlic (*lasan*) paste	6 tsp / 35 gm
Garam masala (see p. 8)	3 tsp / 6 gm
Dry fenugreek leaves (*kasoori methi*), powdered	1 tsp / ½ gm
Tomatoes, deseeded, skinned	350 gm
Salt to taste	
Coriander (*dhaniya*) seeds, roasted, crushed	2 tsp / 6 gm
Black peppercorns (*sabut kali mirch*)	1⅓ tsp / 3 gm
Green chillies, slit	6-8
Green coriander (*hara dhaniya*), chopped	3 tsp / 12 gm

Method

1. Heat the oil; add the dry red chillies and onions. Sauté and then add the ginger-garlic pastes. Cook over medium heat. Add the garam masala, fenugreek powder and tomatoes. Cook over medium heat until the oil separates.

2. Add the morel mushrooms carefully and toss over high heat until the mushrooms are well coated. Cook for 5-6 minutes, stirring occasionally.

3. Add the salt, coriander seeds, black peppercorns, green chillies and green coriander. Serve hot.

Morel mushrooms and corn bonanza

Prep. time: 15 min. • Cooking time: 30 min. • Serves: 4-6

Ingredients

Morel mushrooms (*guchhi*)	500 gm
Sweet corn (*makkai*)	250 gm
Vegetable oil	5 tbsp / 50 ml
Green cardamoms (*choti elaichi*)	4
Cloves (*laung*)	3
Mace (*javitri*) powder	a pinch
Ginger (*adrak*) paste	2 tsp / 12 gm
Garlic (*lasan*) paste	2 tsp / 12 gm
Onion paste	½ cup / 150 gm
Cashew nut (*kaju*) paste	6 tbsp / 60 gm
Yoghurt (*dahi*)	1¼ cups / 375 gm
Green chillies, slit	4
Salt to taste	
Cream	½ cup / 100 gm
Green coriander (*hara dhaniya*), chopped	3 tbsp / 12 gm

Method

1. Heat the oil in a heavy-bottomed pan; add the green cardamoms, cloves and mace powder. When they start crackling, add the ginger and garlic pastes. Mix well. Add the onion and cashew nut pastes. Cook for 5-6 minutes.

2. Add the yoghurt, green chillies, salt, morel mushrooms and corn; simmer for 20 minutes.

3. Mix in the cream and green coriander. Remove and serve with masala *poori* (see p. 183).

Coconut-flavoured fried okra from the south

Prep. time: 30 min. • Cooking time: 30 min. • Serves: 4

Ingredients

Okra (*bhindi*), washed, dried, cut into ½" pieces	800 gm
Vegetable oil for deep-frying	
Cashew nuts (*kaju*)	1 tbsp / 15 gm
Coconut (*nariyal*), grated	⅓ cup / 80 gm
Coconut milk	¼ cup / 60 ml
Cumin (*jeera*) seeds	½ tsp / 1 gm
Mustard seeds (*rai*)	1 tsp / 2 gm
Split black gram (*urad dal*)	4 tsp / 45 gm
Dry red chillies (*sookhi lal mirch*)	3
Curry leaves (*kadhi patta*)	10
Onions, chopped	½ cup / 120 gm
Tomatoes, chopped	240 gm
Red chilli powder	1 tsp / 2 gm
Turmeric (*haldi*) powder	½ tsp / 1 gm
Coriander (*dhaniya*) powder	1 tbsp / 3 gm
Salt to taste	
Yoghurt (*dahi*)	½ cup / 90 gm

Method

1. Heat the oil in a wok (*kadhai*); deep-fry the okra on medium heat for about 5-6 minutes or till crisp. Remove and drain the excess oil on absorbent kitchen towels, reserve the oil.

2. Blend the cashew nuts and coconut in a blender; add coconut milk to make a fine paste. Keep aside.

3. Heat 7 tbsp of the reserved oil; add the cumin seeds,

mustard seeds, black gram, dry red chillies and curry leaves. Sauté over medium heat till the seeds begin to crackle. Add the onions. Sauté till golden brown.

4. Stir in the tomatoes, then add the red chilli powder, turmeric powder, coriander powder and salt. Keep stirring till the oil surfaces.

5. Reduce the flame, add the coconut paste and stir again for 2 minutes. Remove from the fire and mix in the yoghurt. Pour in the water. Return to heat and bring the mixture to the boil. Reduce the flame and simmer. Add the deep-fried okra and cook till the gravy seeps in and the mixture is completely dry.

6. Serve hot.

Recycling Aluminium Foil

Soiled aluminium foil can be
used to scrape burnt food
from pans and dishes.

Crunchy okra

Prep. time: 20 min. • Cooking time: 30 min. • Serves: 4-6

Ingredients

Okra (*bhindi*), cut lengthwise into 4 slices	500 gm
Salt to taste	
Red chilli powder	1 tsp / 2 gm
Garam masala (see p. 8)	1 tsp / 2 gm
Mango powder (*amchur*)	½ tsp / 1 gm
Chaat masala	½ tsp / 1 gm
Gram flour (*besan*)	3 tbsp / 30 gm
Vegetable oil for frying	
Ginger (*adrak*), julienned	1½ tsp / 15 gm
Green chillies, sliced (optional)	2

Method

1. Spread the okra on a flat dish and sprinkle salt, red chilli powder, garam masala, mango powder and *chaat* masala. Mix gently.
2. Now, add the gram flour and mix gently to coat evenly, preferably without adding any water. Divide the okra into 2 portions.
3. Heat the oil in a pan to smoking point. Fry 1 portion of the okra mixture, separating each lightly with a fork. Do not allow the slices to stick to each other. Remove with a slottted spoon when both the sides are crisp and brown. Similarly, fry the other portion.
4. Serve hot garnished with ginger and green chillies.

Cauliflower seasoned with ginger

Prep. time: 10 min. • Cooking time: 25 min. • Serves: 4-5

Ingredients

Cauliflower (*phool gobhi*), cut into florets, washed	1 kg
Vegetable oil	5 tbsp / 50 ml
Onions, finely chopped	³/₄ cup / 180 gm
Ginger (*adrak*) paste	4 tsp / 25 gm
Garlic (*lasan*) paste	4 tsp / 25 gm
Turmeric (*haldi*) powder	2 tsp / 4 gm
Red chilli powder	2 tsp / 4 gm
White pepper (*safed mirch*) powder	1 tsp / 2 gm
Coriander (*dhaniya*) powder	2 tsp / 3 gm
Tomatoes, skinned, chopped	100 gm
Salt to taste	
Garam masala (see p. 8)	2 tsp / 4 gm
Butter	2 tsp / 10 gm
Ginger (*adrak*), julienned	2 tsp / 15 gm
Green coriander (*hara dhaniya*), chopped	2 tsp / 4 gm

Method

1. Heat the oil in a pan, add the onions and sauté over medium heat. Add the ginger-garlic pastes, turmeric, red chilli, white pepper, coriander powders and tomatoes. Sauté for a minute.
2. Add the cauliflower and ¹/₂ cup water. Cover and cook for 15 minutes till the mixture is absolutely dry. Season with salt and garam masala.
3. Heat the butter in a pan; add the ginger and sauté lightly. Remove and sprinkle over the cauliflower. Garnish with green coriander.

Baked spicy cauliflower

Prep. time: 15 min. ● Cooking time: 30 min. ● Serves: 4

Ingredients

Cauliflower (*phool gobhi*), cut into florets	175 gm
Turmeric (*haldi*) powder	a pinch
Salt to taste	
Bay leaves (*tej patta*)	4
Water as required	
Vegetable oil	2 tbsp / 20 ml
Cloves (*laung*)	4
Green cardamoms (*choti elaichi*)	4
Ginger-garlic (*adrak-lasan*) paste	2 tsp / 12 gm
Butter	3 tbsp / 60 gm
Garam masala (see p. 8)	a pinch
Red chilli powder	a pinch
White pepper (*safed mirch*) powder	a pinch
Cashew nut (*kaju*) paste	3 tbsp / 30 gm
Yoghurt (*dahi*)	2 tbsp / 60 gm
Tomato purée, fresh	3 tbsp / 45 gm
Brown onion paste	3¹/₃ tbsp / 50 gm
Cream	¹/₄ cup / 50 gm

Method

1. Boil the water in a pan; add the turmeric powder, salt and bay leaves. Gradually, add the cauliflower and cook covered on medium heat till ¾th done.
2. Remove from heat and drain the water. Transfer the cauliflower to an ovenproof dish.
3. Heat the oil in a pan; add the cloves and green

cardamoms. Sauté till they crackle. Stir in the ginger-garlic paste dissolved in 2 tbsp water. When the water dries out, add the butter and the spices.

4. Mix the cashew nut paste and yoghurt in ½ cup water and add to the pan. Cook on low heat till it comes to the boil. Stir in the tomato purée and the brown onion paste. Cook covered for about 5 minutes and stir in the cream.

5. Remove from heat and pour over the cauliflower florets.

6. Bake in a moderately hot oven for about 5-10 minutes and serve hot.

Easy Peel
Garlic cloves can be peeled easily if
they are soaked in a little water.

Cauliflower and peas delight

Phool Gobhi Kerau

Prep. time: 15 min. ● Cooking time: 15 min. ● Serves: 4-6

Ingredients

Cauliflower (*phool gobhi*), cut into medium-sized florets	750 gm
Green peas (*mattar*), shelled	200 gm
Mustard (*sarson*) oil	4 tbsp / 40 ml
Fenugreek seeds (*methi dana*)	1 tsp / 3 gm
Turmeric (*haldi*) powder	1/2 tsp / 1 gm
Salt to taste	
Garlic (*lasan*), peeled, crushed	1 tbsp / 18 gm
Ginger (*adrak*), scraped, finely ground	2 tsp / 12 gm
Green chillies, slit, deseeded	6-7

Method

1. Slit the stalks of the florets and immerse in water. Mix 1/2 tsp salt with the green peas.
2. Heat the mustard oil in a pan; add the fenugreek seeds. When it crackles, add the drained florets. Cook covered till soft.
3. Add the turmeric powder and toss. After 2 minutes, add salt and cook covered for 5 more minutes till the cauliflower becomes tender. If still not tender, sprinkle a little water and cook, covered again.
4. Add the garlic, ginger, green chillies and peas and cook covered, stirring occasionally till the peas turn tender and the oil separates.
5. Serve hot.

Prep. time: 45 min. • Cooking time: 30 min. • Serves: 4

Ingredients

French beans, chopped	120 gm
Cabbage (*bandh gobhi*), chopped	120 gm
Capsicum (*Shimla mirch*), chopped	120 gm
Carrots (*gajar*), chopped	120 gm
Onions, chopped	½ cup / 120 gm
Potatoes, cut into fingers	120 gm
Vegetable oil	4 tbsp / 40 ml
Cumin (*jeera*) seeds	1 tsp / 2 gm
Dry red chillies (*sookhi lal mirch*)	2
Salt to taste	
Black pepper (*kali mirch*) powder	½ tsp / 1 gm
Ginger (*adrak*), chopped	2 tsp / 20 gm
Tomato purée	4 tbsp / 80 gm
White vinegar	1 tbsp / 15 ml
Green coriander (*hara dhaniya*), chopped	1 tbsp / 4 gm

Method

1. Heat the oil in a pan; add the cumin seeds and dry red chillies. Sauté for a few seconds. Add all the vegetables, salt, black pepper powder and ginger. Mix well. Cook covered on a slow fire till the vegetables are almost tender.

2. Add the tomato purée and white vinegar. Cook till the vegetables are completely done. Remove from the fire.

3. Serve hot garnished with green coriander.

Mixed vegetables flavoured with coconut

Prep. time: 45 min. • Cooking time: 30 min. • Serves: 4

Ingredients

French beans, chopped	100 gm
Carrots (*gajar*), diced	100 gm
Kohlrabi (*ganth gobhi*), dried	100 gm
Green peas (*mattar*), shelled	100 gm
Potatoes, diced	100 gm
Tomatoes, chopped	100 gm
Coconut (*nariyal*), grated	$^2/_3$ cup / 160 gm
Green chillies, chopped	2
Onions, chopped	2 tbsp / 25 gm
Ginger (*adrak*), chopped	1 tsp / 10 gm
Turmeric (*haldi*) powder	$^1/_2$ tsp / 1 gm
Green coriander (*hara dhaniya*), chopped	2 tsp / 4 gm
Fennel (*saunf*) seeds	2 tsp / 3 gm
Cinnamon (*dalchini*), 1" stick	1
Cloves (*laung*)	3
Green cardamoms (*choti elaichi*)	6
Poppy seeds (*khuskhus*)	2 tsp / 6 gm
Bay leaves (*tej patta*)	2
Salt to taste	
Ghee	2 tbsp / 30 gm

Method

1. Blend the coconut, green chillies, onions, ginger, turmeric powder and green coriander to a fine paste in a blender.

2. On a hot griddle, roast the fennel seeds, cinnamon

stick, cloves, green cardamoms and poppy seeds. When cool, blend to make a fine powder.

3. Heat a pan, add all the vegetables and pour just enough water to cover the vegetables. Add the bay leaves and salt; cook till the vegetables are tender and the water has dried up. Stir in the coconut-onion paste and cook for 2-3 minutes.

4. Add the powdered spices and ghee. Stir well for 5 minutes.

5. Serve hot.

Preserving Spices

Coriander powder and other spices will preserve well if a few pieces of asafoetida (hing) is put in them.

Nepalese-style mixed vegetable

Prep. time: 20 min. ● Cooking time: 20 min. ● Serves: 4-6

Ingredients

Potatoes, peeled, cubed, washed,	500 gm
Mustard (*sarson*) oil	1 cup / 170 ml
Asafoetida (*hing*)	a pinch
Fenugreek seeds (*methi dana*)	$\frac{1}{2}$ tsp / 1$\frac{1}{2}$ gm
Timmur (see front cover flap), optional	4-5 grains
Garlic (*lasan*) cloves, pounded	2 tsp / 6 gm
Turmeric (*haldi*) powder	$\frac{1}{2}$ tsp / 1 gm
Salt to taste	
Onions, peeled, quartered	125 gm
Green peas (*mattar*), peeled	200 gm
Capsicum (*Shimla mirch*), cut into long strips	1

Grind together:

Coriander (*dhaniya*) seeds	2 tsp / 6 gm
Black cumin (*shah jeera*) seeds	1 tsp / 2 gm
Black pepper (*kali mirch*) powder	$\frac{1}{2}$ tsp / 1 gm
Red chilli powder	2 tsp / 4 gm
Ginger (*adrak*), ground	1 tsp / 6 gm

Yoghurt (*dahi*)	$\frac{1}{2}$ cup / 90 gm
Tomatoes, medium-sized, quartered	4
Fresh bamboo shoots, cubed	20 gm
Spring onions, cut into slices with green stems	2
Green coriander (*hara dhaniya*)	1 tbsp / 4 gm

Method

1. Immerse the potatoes in water and keep aside.
2. Heat the oil in a pan; add the asafoetida, fenugreek seeds and *timmur*. Stir for a few seconds. Then add garlic and fry till light brown.
3. Add the drained potatoes, turmeric powder and salt. Stir occasionally.
4. Once the potatoes are half done, add the onions and cook for 5 minutes. Add the green peas and capsicum. Sprinkle more water, if required, and cook covered for 5 minutes.
5. Add the ground spices mixed with yoghurt. Mix well and cook further for 3 more minutes.
6. Add the tomatoes, bamboo shoots, spring onions and ½ cup water. Simmer till there is very little water left. Serve hot.

Cold Relief
For instant relief from cold, add
1 tsp of turmeric powder
(haldi) to a glass of hot milk
and drink it.

A traditionally cooked aubergine delight

Prep. time: 10 min. • Cooking time: 1 hr. • Serves: 4

Ingredients

Aubergine (*baingan*), approx ½ kg	1
Vegetable oil	2 tbsp / 20 ml
Cumin (*jeera*) seeds	¼ tsp / 1gm
Spring onions or ordinary onions (minced)	3
Garlic (*lasan*), crushed	1 tsp / 3 gm
Green chillies, sliced	2
Salt to taste	
Yoghurt (*dahi*)	1 cup / 180 gm
Garam masala (see p. 8)	1 tsp / 2 gm
Green coriander (*hara dhaniya*), chopped	1 tsp / 2 gm

Method

1. Cut the aubergine lengthwise into half. Cover with a foil and bake in a moderately hot oven (175°C / 350°F) for 40 minutes or until tender. When cool, remove the skin and mash the flesh of the aubergine.
2. Heat the oil in a wok (*kadhai*); add the cumin seeds and sauté until dark brown. Add the minced onions and fry until golden brown.
3. Add the garlic, green chillies, aubergine and cook on a low flame for 15-20 minutes.
4. Add salt and yoghurt, cook on medium heat for another 5-8 minutes, stirring occasionally. Mix in the garam masala and green coriander.
5. Serve hot.

Fried aubergine – Bengali style

Prep. time: 30 min. ● Cooking time: 15 min. ● Serves: 2-4

Ingredients

Aubergines (*baingan*), large, cut into quarters | 4
Salt to taste
Turmeric (*haldi*) powder | 2 tsp / 4 gm
Mustard (sarson) oil | ½ cup / 85 ml

Method

1. Rub the aubergines with salt and turmeric powder. Keep aside for ½ an hour.
2. Heat the mustard oil in a shallow pan; fry the aubergines till golden brown. Remove with a slotted spoon and drain the excess oil on absorbent kitchen towels.
3. Serve immediately.

Better Buy

Buy aubergines that are heavy, firm, free from blemish and of uniform dark colour. Avoid buying the ones that have dark brown spots on the surface as they indicate decay.

Aubergines with tender neem leaves

Prep. time: 15 min. • Cooking time: 30 min. • Serves: 2-4

Ingredients

Aubergines (*baingan*), diced	150 gm
Tender neem leaves	50 gm
Salt to taste	
Turmeric (*haldi*) powder	1 tsp / 2 gm
Mustard (*sarson*) oil	1/4 cup / 50 ml

Method

1. Marinate the aubergines with salt and turmeric powder for 15 minutes.
2. Heat the oil in a wok (*kadhai*); deep-fry the aubergines till crisp. Keep aside.
3. In the same oil, deep-fry the neem leaves. Keep aside.
4. Mix the two together and serve with steamed rice and ghee.

Ennai Kathirikkai

Prep. time: 30 min. • Cooking time: 20 min. • Serves: 4

Ingredients

Aubergines (*baingan*), small, slit into 4, with stems intact	450 gm
Coconut (*nariyal*), grated, roasted	$^2/_3$ cup / 160 gm
Bengal gram (*chana dal*)	$^1/_2$ tbsp / 12 gm
Split black gram (*urad dal*)	I tbsp / 20 gm
Tamarind (*imli*) extract	2 tsp / 10 gm
Vegetable oil	$^2/_3$ cup / 115 gm
Mustard (*sarson*) seeds	$^1/_2$ tsp / I gm
Curry leaves (*kadhi patta*)	10
Asafoetida (*hing*)	a pinch
Coriander (*dhaniya*) seeds	I tbsp / 5 gm
Cumin (*jeera*) seeds	I tbsp / 8 gm
Dry red chillies (*sookhi lal mirch*)	4
Salt to taste	
Water	$^1/_2$ cup / 100 ml

Method

1. Roast half the Bengal and black gram till light brown. Then blend them with the roasted coconut and tamarind extract. Use 2 tbsp water, if necessary. Fill the aubergines with this paste.

2. Heat the oil; add mustard seeds, the remaining Bengal and black gram, curry leaves and asafoetida. When the seeds begin to crackle, add the remaining spices, the stuffed aubergines and the leftover paste, if any. Add the water. Stir for 2-3 minutes, cover and simmer over gentle heat till the aubergines are tender.

Cabbage stir-fried with coconut

Prep. time: 20 min. • Cooking time: 30 min. • Serves: 4

Ingredients

Cabbage (*bandh gobhi*), chopped	500 gm
Vegetable oil	3 tbsp / 30 ml
Mustard seeds (*rai*)	$1/2$ tsp / 1 gm
Cumin (*jeera*) seeds	$1/2$ tsp / 1 gm
Split black gram (*urad dal*)	2 tsp / 20 gm
Dry red chilli (*sookhi lal mirch*)	1
Asafoetida (*hing*)	a pinch
Curry leaves (*kadhi patta*)	10
Green chillies, slit	2
Green peas (*mattar*), shelled	150 gm
Salt to taste	
Coconut (*nariyal*), grated	2 tbsp / 8 gm

Method

1. Heat the oil in a wok (*kadhai*); add the mustard seeds, cumin seeds, split black gram, dry red chilli, asafoetida and curry leaves.
2. When the seeds begin to crackle, add green chillies, cabbage, green peas and salt.
3. Stir well. Cook covered over gentle heat till the vegetables are tender. Mix in the coconut.
4. Serve hot with parathas.

Note: Other vegetables such as carrots, beet root or cauliflower can be used instead of the green ones used in this recipe.

French beans stir-fried with coconut

Prep. time: 25 min. • Cooking time: 20 min. • Serves: 4-5

Ingredients

French beans, strings removed, finely chopped	1 kg
Turmeric (*haldi*) powder	½ tsp / 1 gm
Salt to taste	
Vegetable oil	4 tbsp / 40 ml
Mustard seeds (*rai*)	1 tsp / 3 gm
Split black gram (*urad dal*)	1 tsp / 5 gm
Dry red chillies (*sookhi lal mirch*)	2
Onions, chopped	2
Green chillies, chopped	2
Coconut (*nariyal*), fresh, grated	½

Method

1. Boil the French beans in 1 cup water with turmeric powder and salt. Cook until the beans are almost done. Drain and keep aside.

2. Heat the oil in a wok (*kadhai*); add the mustard seeds, split black gram and dry red chillies. When the mustard seeds begin to crackle, add the onions and green chillies. Sauté for 4-5 minutes.

3. Add the beans and stir-fry till well mixed. Stir in the salt and coconut, mix well and remove from the fire.

4. Serve immediately with a curry dish and steamed rice.

Stir-fried peas

Prep. time: 20 min. • Cooking time: 10 min. • Serves: 4-6

Ingredients

Green peas (*mattar*), shelled, washed, dried	500 gm
Vegetable oil	1 tbsp / 10 ml
Asafoetida (*hing*)	a pinch
Green chillies, chopped	2
Mango powder (*amchur*)	1 tsp / 2 gm
Red chilli powder	½ tsp / 1 gm
Salt to taste	
Garam masala (see p. 8)	1 tsp / 2 gm
Green coriander (*hara dhaniya*), chopped	1 tbsp / 4 gm

Method

1. Heat the oil in a deep pan; add the asafoetida. Stir for a few seconds then mix in the green chillies and green peas. Cover the pan and cook on low heat for at least 8-10 minutes or until almost cooked.

2. Add the mango powder, red chilli powder, salt and garam masala. Stir and continue to cook for 3-4 minutes. Remove from the fire, transfer the contents on to a flat serving dish, garnish with green coriander and serve very hot.

Spicy garlic-flavoured peas – Nepalese style

Prep. time: 20 min. • Serves: 4-6

Ingredients

Green peas (*mattar*), shelled	2 cups
Salt to taste	
Green garlic (*hara lasan*) with stems, dry roasted, chopped	2 bunches / 20 pods
Cumin (*jeera*) seeds, roasted, ground	2 tsp / 1 gm
Dry red chillies (*sookhi lal mirch*), roasted, coarsely ground	10 gm
Ginger (*adrak*), grated, dry roasted	2 tsp / 20 gm
Chukamilo (see front cover flap)	1/4 tsp
or	
Lemon (*nimbu*) juice	2 tsp / 10 ml
Green chillies, dry roasted,	

Method

1. Mix the salt with the peas and keep aside for 30 minutes.
2. Combine all the ingredients and mix well with the peas.
3. Serve cold.

Spiced green pumpkin – Nepalese style

Prep. time: 20 min. ● Cooking time: 20 min. ● Serves: 2-4

Ingredients

Green pumpkin (*hara kaddu*), deseeded	I kg
Mustard (*sarson*) oil	3 tbsp / 30 ml
Asafoetida (*hing*)	a pinch
Fenugreek seeds (*methi dana*)	I tsp / 3 gm
Turmeric (*haldi*) powder	¹/₂ tsp / I gm
Salt to taste	
Green chillies, chopped	4-5
Garlic (*lasan*), peeled, crushed	2 tsp / 6 gm
Cumin (*jeera*) powder	¹/₂ tsp / I gm
Coriander (*dhaniya*) powder	¹/₂ tsp / I gm

Method

1. Dice / grate the pumpkin without peeling it.
2. Heat the oil in a pan; add the asafoetida and fenugreek seeds. Sauté for a few seconds. Add the pumpkin and cook covered for 10 minutes.
3. Add the turmeric powder and salt. Toss a little and then add green chillies and garlic. Cook further for 3-4 minutes, tossing occasionally.
4. Add the cumin powder and coriander powder. Mix well and cook covered for 3-4 minutes on a low flame.
5. Remove and serve hot.

Nepalese hot and sour pumpkin

Prep. time: 10 min. • Cooking time: 20 min. • Serves: 2-4

Ingredients

Red pumpkin (*lal kaddu*), peeled, sliced	500 gm
Mustard (*sarson*) oil	3 tbsp / 30 ml
Fenugreek seeds (*methi dana*)	1 tsp / 2 gm
Salt to taste	
Turmeric (*haldi*) powder	½ tsp / 1 gm
Garlic (*lasan*) cloves, crushed	6-7
Ginger (*adrak*), scraped, ground	1 tsp / 6 gm
Green chillies, quartered, deseeded	4
Lapsi*	6
Cumin (*jeera*) seeds, dry roasted	1 tsp / 2 gm
Coriander (*dhaniya*) seeds, dry roasted, powdered	2 tsp / 4 gm

Method

1. Heat the mustard oil; add the fenugreek seeds. When it starts crackling, add the red pumpkin, salt and turmeric powder. Cook till the water is absorbed. Add the garlic, ginger, green chillies and 2 tbsp water. Mix well.

2. Add the *lapsi* and cook for 10 minutes or till the pumpkin is soft and the *lapsi* tender.

3. Now add the dry powdered spices and sprinkle 2 tbsp water and cook till the pumpkin is pulpy in appearance. Serve hot.

Note: **Lapsi* is a roundish wild fruit with a thick skin and sour pulp.

Raw papaya – a Bengali favourite

Prep. time: 20 min. ● Cooking time: 30 min. ● Serves: 2-4

Ingredients

Raw papaya (*papita*), diced	300 gm
Vegetable oil	2 tbsp / 20 ml
Panch phoran (see p. 8)	2 tsp / 10 gm
Bay leaf (*tej patta*)	1
Turmeric (*haldi*) powder	1 tsp / 2 gm
Ginger (*adrak*) paste	1 tsp / 6 gm
Red chilli powder	1 tsp / 2 gm
Green chillies, chopped	2
Tomatoes, chopped	50 gm
Water	1 cup / 200 ml
Salt to taste	

Method

1. Heat the oil in a wok (*kadhai*); add the *panch phoran* and bay leaf. Let it crackle for a while.
2. Add the raw papaya and sauté; add the turmeric powder, ginger paste, red chilli powder, green chillies and tomatoes.
3. Add the water and salt. Cook till the water is completely absorbed and the papaya is soft.
4. Serve hot.

Rajasthani spicy corn

Prep. time: 20 min. • Cooking time: 30 min. • Serves: 2-4

Ingredients

Corn (*makkai*) kernels, coarsely grated	500 gm
Vegetable oil	5 tbsp / 50 ml
Cumin (*jeera*) seeds	½ tsp / 1 gm
Onion, finely chopped	1
Ginger (*adrak*) paste	1½ tsp / 9 gm
Garlic (*lasan*) paste	1½ tsp / 9 gm
Turmeric (*haldi*) powder	½ tsp / 1 gm
Salt to taste	
Red chilli powder	½ tsp / 1 gm
Coriander (*dhaniya*) powder	1 tsp / 2 gm
Water	2½ cups / 500 ml
Cream, whipped	½ cup / 100 gm
Green coriander (*hara dhaniya*), chopped	1 tbsp / 4 gm

Method

1. Heat the oil in a pan; add the cumin seeds and onions. Sauté till the onions turn golden. Add the ginger and garlic pastes. Cook until brown.

2. Mix the turmeric powder, salt, red chilli powder and coriander powder in ½ cup water and add to the onion mixture. Cook for 5 minutes on a low flame. Add the corn and fry for 5 minutes. Pour the remaining water and cook covered on a low flame for 10-12 minutes. When the corn is tender and the mixture is dry, mix in the cream.

3. Serve hot garnished with green coriander.

Stir-fried corn

Prep. time: 15 min. • Cooking time: 20 min. • Serves: 2-4

Ingredients

Corn (*makkai*) kernels, separated	8
Vegetable oil	2 tbsp / 20 ml
Asafoetida (*hing*)	a small pinch
Cumin (*jeera*) seeds	1 tsp / 2 gm
Black peppercorns (*sabut kali mirch*), pounded	½ tsp / 1 gm
Ginger-garlic (*adrak-lasan*) paste	1 tsp / 6 gm
Green chillies, chopped	2-3
Turmeric (*haldi*) powder	½ tsp / 1 gm
Salt to taste	
Garam masala (see p. 8)	½ tsp / 1 gm
Cumin (*jeera*) powder	½ tsp / 1 gm
Lemon (*nimbu*), cut into wedges	1
Green coriander (*hara dhaniya*), chopped	1 tbsp / 4 gm

Method

1. Heat the oil in a wok (*kadhai*); add asafoetida and cumin seeds. When they start crackling, add the black peppercorns and ginger-garlic paste. Sauté for a while.
2. Add the corn kernels, green chillies, turmeric powder and salt. Stir and add the cumin powder with 1 tbsp water. Cook covered on a low flame, till the mixture is dry and the corns are tender.
3. Serve hot garnished with lemon wedges and green coriander.

Makkai Tareko

Spicy green tomatoes – Rajasthani style

Prep. time: 15 min. • Cooking time: 20 min. • Serves: 2-4

Ingredients

Green tomatoes, cut into big pieces	500 gm
Vegetable oil	¼ cup / 45 ml
Cumin (*jeera*) seeds	½ tsp / 1 gm
Fenugreek seeds (*methi dana*)	½ tsp / 1½ gm
Green chillies, slit	2-3
Red chilli powder	1 tsp / 2 gm
Coriander (*dhaniya*) powder	2 tsp / 3 gm
Turmeric (*haldi*) powder	½ tsp / 1 gm
Mango powder (*amchur*)	½ tsp / 1 gm
Salt to taste	
Sugar	a pinch
Garlic (*lasan*) paste	1 tsp / 6 gm

Method

1. Heat the oil in a wok (*kadhai*); add the cumin and fenugreek seeds. When they start to crackle, add the green tomatoes and green chillies. Fry for 1-2 minutes.
2. Add all the dry spices, salt and sugar. Cook covered for 5-6 minutes, or till the tomatoes lose their shape. Add the garlic paste and stir-fry for 2-3 minutes.
3. Serve hot.

Hare Tamatar ki Sabzi

A Rajasthani green chilli preparation

Prep. time: 15 min. • Cooking time: 30 min. • Serves: 2-4

Ingredients

Green chillies, large, slit	500 gm
Gram flour (besan)	1/2 cup / 50 gm
Salt to taste	
Red chilli powder	1/2 tsp / 1 gm
Turmeric (haldi) powder	1/4 tsp / 1/4 gm
Coriander (dhaniya) powder	1/2 tsp / 1 gm
Mango powder (amchur)	1 tsp / 2 gm
Water	1/4 cup / 50 ml
Vegetable oil	1/2 cup / 85 ml

Method

1. Roast the gram flour in a wok (kadhai) for 5 minutes or till it emanates a roasted fragrance.
2. Add all the dry spices and water and cook till a thick paste-like consistency is obtained. Stir continuously. Remove from the flame and keep aside to cool.
3. Stuff the green chillies with this gram flour paste.
4. Heat the oil in a wok; fry the green chillies on a low flame till tender and brown. Remove from the flame and serve hot.

Lotus root roganjosh

Prep. time: 10 min. • Cooking time: 30 min. • Serves: 2-4

Ingredients

Lotus root (*kamal kakri*), scraped, cut into 2" pieces and then halved	500 gm
Vegetable oil	5 tbsp / 50 ml
Cumin (*jeera*) seeds	½ tsp / 1 gm
Cloves (*laung*)	3
Bay leaves (*tej patta*)	2
Black cardamoms (*badi elaichi*), crushed	2
Salt to taste	
Asafoetida (*hing*)	a pinch
Red chilli powder	1 tsp / 2 gm
Yoghurt (*dahi*)	2 tbsp / 60 gm
Water	1½ cups / 300 ml
Ginger powder (*moti sonth*)	1 tsp / 2 gm
Aniseed (*moti saunf*), powdered	2 tsp / 3 gm
Garam masala (see p. 8)	½ tsp / 1 gm

Method

1. Heat the oil in a pan; add the cumin seeds, cloves, bay leaves and black cardamoms. When they start crackling, add the lotus root, salt and asafoetida. Sauté over low heat for about 7 minutes, stirring continuously.

2. Add the red chilli powder mixed with yoghurt. Stir vigorously for 30 seconds over a high flame. Add water and bring the mixture to the boil. Add the remaining ingredients. Cook for 10-15 minutes or till the water is absorbed. Serve hot.

Kashmiri mashed turnip

Prep. time: 10 min. • Cooking time: 20 min. • Serves: 4-6

Ingredients

Turnips (*shalgam*), washed, cut into thick, wafer-like slices	500 gm
Vegetable oil	3 tbsp / 30 ml
Asafoetida (*hing*)	a pinch
Sugar	a pinch
Salt to taste	
Dry red chillies (*sookhi lal mirch*), deseeded, halved	3
Tikki masala, crushed (see p. 8)	1/2 tsp / 1 gm
Water	1/2 cup / 100 ml

Method

1. Heat the oil in a heavy-bottomed pan; add the turnips, asafoetida, sugar and salt.
2. Add the dry red chillies and stir well. Cook covered over a high flame for 5 minutes.
3. Lower the flame, stirring often to ensure that the mixture doesn't stick to the bottom of the pan.
4. Add the *tikki* masala and water. Stir well. Lightly mash the turnips with the back of the ladle, while stirring. Cook till the mixture is almost dry.
5. Serve hot with rice and plain yoghurt.

Spicy chickpea

Prep. time: 3¼ hrs. • Cooking time: 1 hr. • Serves: 4

Ingredients

Chickpea (kabuli chana), soaked for 3 hours	250 gm
Water	10 cups / 2 lt
Bay leaf (tej patta)	1
Cinnamon (dalchini), 1" sticks	3
Cardamoms (claichi), green or black	3
Tea bag	1
Bicarbonate of soda	1 tsp / 6 gm
Vegetable oil	4 tbsp / 40 ml
Ginger (adrak) paste	2 tsp / 12 gm
Garlic (lasan) paste	2 tsp / 12 gm
Red chilli powder	¾ tsp / 2 gm
Garam masala (see p. 8)	1 tsp / 2 gm
Coriander (dhaniya) powder	1 tsp / 2 gm
Chana masala	1 tsp / 2 gm
Salt to taste	
Lemon (nimbu) juice	1 tbsp / 15 ml
For the garnish:	
Green chillies, whole	10
Lemons, cut into wedges	3
Onion, cut into rings	1
Tomatoes, medium-sized, quartered	50 gm

Method

1. In a heavy pot, pour the water and bring it to boil. Add the bay leaf, cinnamon sticks, green or black cardamoms, tea bag and chickpea and let it boil. Add

the bicarbonate of soda. Cover and cook over low heat until tender. Drain immediately. Remove the bay leaf, tea bag, cinnamon sticks and cardamoms.

2. Heat the oil in a pan over low heat. Add the ginger and garlic pastes and sauté for 30-40 seconds. Add the red chilli powder, garam masala, coriander powder, *chana* masala, salt and lemon juice. Add the drained and boiled chickpea and mix carefully.

3. Serve hot garnished with green chillies, lemon wedges, onion rings and tomatoes.

Free Flowing

*Put small pieces of blotting paper at
the bottom of a silver salt shaker.
This will absorb the moisture in the
salt and keep it running freely.*

Curries

Minced peas and potatoes

Prep. time: 10 min. • Cooking time: 30 min. • Serves: 4-6

Ingredients

Green peas (*mattar*), minced	300 gm
Potatoes, small, diced	5-6
Green chillies, chopped	1-2
Ginger (*adrak*), chopped	1½" piece
Tomatoes, chopped	400 gm
Ghee, melted	½ cup / 80 gm
Cumin (*jeera*) seeds	1½ tsp / 3 gm
Cloves (*laung*), ground	6
Cinnamon (*dalchini*), 1" sticks, ground	2
Black peppercorns (*sabut kali mirch*), ground	6-8
Coriander (*dhaniya*) powder	1 tsp / 1½ gm
Turmeric (*haldi*) powder	1 tsp / 2 gm
Red chilli powder	½ tsp / 1 gm
Salt to taste	
Garam masala (see p. 8)	3 tsp / 6 gm
Green coriander (*hara dhaniya*), chopped	2 tbsp / 8 gm

Method

1. Blend the green chillies, ginger and tomatoes together.
2. Heat 4 tbsp ghee in a wok (*kadhai*); add the minced peas and fry till the oil separates.
3. Heat 2 tbsp ghee; add the cumin seeds. When it crackles, add the fried peas, and all the spices and condiments. Sauté, add the green chilli purée and bring to the boil. Add potatoes and cook till tender. Add salt and garam masala. Garnish with green coriander.

Stuffed potatoes in a green curry

Prep. time: 45 min. ● Cooking time: 1 hr. ● Serves: 4

Ingredients

Potatoes, medium-sized, round	I kg
Vegetable oil for frying	
Mint (pudina) leaves	3 tbsp / 12 gm
Green coriander (hara dhaniya)	6 tbsp / 24 gm
Green chillies, chopped	10
Cumin (jeera) seeds	½ tsp / I gm
Mango powder (amchur)	I tsp / 2 gm
Raisins (kishmish)	4 tsp / 12 gm
Salt to taste	
Vegetable oil	6 tbsp / 60 ml
Turmeric (haldi) powder	½ tsp / I gm
Tomatoes, chopped	80 gm
Spinach (palak), chopped	400 gm
Fenugreek leaves (methi), chopped	3½ cups / 105 gm
Red chilli powder	2 tsp / 4 gm
Yoghurt (dahi)	3 tbsp / 90 gm
Garam masala (see p. 8)	I tsp / 2 gm
Coriander (dhaniya) powder	I tsp / 2 gm
Ghee	2 tbsp / 30 gm

Method

1. Peel and scoop out the inside portion of the potatoes and deep fry the potato shells till crisp and golden brown.

2. Grind the mint leaves, green coriander, green chillies, cumin seeds, mango powder, raisins and salt together with very little water to make a fine paste. Keep aside.

3. Heat the oil in a wok (*kadhai*); add the turmeric powder, tomatoes, spinach and fenugreek leaves. Sauté lightly.

4. Add the red chilli powder and salt; cook till the curry thickens. Mix in the yoghurt, garam masala, coriander powder and ghee. Remove from heat and keep aside to cool.

5. When the mixture is cool enough, blend to a thick gravy and reheat.

6. Spoon the prepared gravy into the fried potato shells. Place the stuffed potatoes in a shallow dish and pour the leftover gravy over them.

7. Serve hot.

Nutritious Water

Do not throw the water in which
the vegetables have been boiled.
This water has high nutritive value.
Use it for kneading the dough.

Stuffed potato bonanza

Prep. time: 20 min. • Cooking time: 20 min. • Serves: 4-5

Ingredients

Potatoes, small, round, boiled, peeled	600 gm
For the filling:	
Ghee	1 tbsp / 15 gm
Onions, grated	51/3 tbsp / 130 gm
Ginger (*adrak*) paste	2 tbsp / 36 gm
Garlic (*lasan*) paste	2 tbsp / 36 gm
Potatoes, boiled, grated	200 gm
Red chilli powder	2 tsp / 4 gm
Turmeric (*haldi*) powder	1 tsp / 2 gm
Garam masala (see p. 8)	2 tsp / 4 gm
Lemon (*nimbu*) juice	1 tbsp / 15 ml
Salt to taste	
For the gravy:	
Vegetable oil	3¹/₃ tbsp / 35 ml
Bay leaf (*tej patta*)	1
Cinnamon (*dalchini*), 1" sticks	2
Cloves (*laung*)	6
Green cardamoms (*choti elaichi*)	6
Black cumin (*shah jeera*) seeds	²/₃ tsp / 2 gm
Turmeric (*haldi*) powder	a pinch
Red chilli powder	a pinch
Yoghurt (*dahi*), whisked	¾ cup / 225 gm
Garam masala (see p. 8)	a pinch
Salt to taste	
Lemon (*nimbu*) juice	a few drops
Ginger (*adrak*), julienned	

Method

1. **For the filling**, heat the ghee in a pan; add half of the onion, ginger and garlic pastes and fry for 4-5 minutes. Add the potatoes, red chilli powder, turmeric powder and garam masala. Season with lemon juice and salt. Keep aside.
2. Scoop out the inside portion of the potatoes and deep-fry the shells till slightly crisp. Keep aside to cool.
3. When cool enough to handle, fill each potato shell with the potato mixture. Cover and keep aside.
4. **For the gravy**, heat the oil in a pan over medium heat. Add the bay leaf, cinnamon sticks, cloves, green cardamoms, black cumin seeds and fry until they crackle. Mix in the remaining onion, ginger and garlic pastes, stir-fry for 2-3 minutes.
5. Add the turmeric powder and red chilli powder, stir-fry over medium heat for 5-6 minutes. Stir in the yoghurt. Cook till the mixture is dry, stirring regularly. Sprinkle garam masala and season with salt.
6. Arrange the stuffed potatoes in the pan with the gravy. Sprinkle some lemon juice and cook covered for 3-4 minutes on very low heat.
7. Serve hot garnished with ginger and accompanied with rice.

Nepalese potato and tomato curry

Prep. time: 20 min. ● Cooking time: 20 min. ● Serves: 2-4

Ingredients

Potatoes, peeled, cubed	500 gm
Tomatoes, diced	250 gm
Mustard (sarson) oil	4 tbsp / 40 ml
Asafoetida (hing)	a pinch
Fenugreek seeds (methi dana)	1/2 tsp / 1 1/2 gm
Cumin (jeera) seeds	1/2 tsp / 1 gm
Turmeric (haldi) powder	1/2 tsp / 1 gm
Salt to taste	
Ginger (adrak), ground	1 tsp / 6 gm
Garlic (lasan), pound	2 tsp / 12 gm
Tomatoes, medium-sized, chopped	2
Green chillies, slit	5-6
Coriander (dhaniya) powder	2 tsp / 4 gm
Garam masala (see p. 8)	1 tsp / 2 gm
Water	2 cups / 400 ml
Green coriander (hara dhaniya), chopped	1 tbsp / 4 gm

Method

1. Heat the mustard oil in a pan; add asafoetida, fenugreek seeds and cumin seeds. When they crackle, mix in the potatoes, turmeric powder and salt.

2. Now, add ginger and garlic, stir for a minute. Add the remaining ingredients (except green coriander) and boil till the vegetables are cooked. Stir well, crushing the vegetables with the back of the spoon to thicken the gravy. Add the green coriander, cook for 2 minutes and serve hot.

Bengali potato and cauliflower curry

Prep. time: 20 min. • Cooking time: 30 min. • Serves: 2-4

Ingredients

Potatoes, cut into wedges	200 gm
Cauliflower (*phool gobhi*), cut into florets	100 gm
Vegetable oil	¼ cup / 45 ml
Cinnamon (*dalchini*), 1" stick	1
Coriander (*dhaniya*) powder	1 tsp / 2 gm
Red chilli powder	1 tsp / 2 gm
Cumin (*jeera*) powder	1 tsp / 2 gm
Ginger (*adrak*) paste	2 tsp / 12 gm
Tomatoes, chopped	50 gm
Water	2 cups / 400 ml

Method

1. Heat the oil in a wok (*kadhai*); add the cinnamon stick, coriander powder, red chilli powder and cumin powder. Stir for a few seconds.
2. Add the potatoes. Cook over a high flame, until the potatoes are almost done. Add the ginger paste and tomatoes. Cook for 5 minutes over a medium flame. Add the cauliflower and water.
3. Cook over a low flame till the cauliflower is done.
4. Serve hot.

Jackfruit and potato curry

Prep. time: 40 min. ● Cooking time: 40 min. ● Serves: 2-4

Ingredients

Jackfruit (*kathal*), diced	300 gm
Potatoes, diced	150 gm
Vegetable oil	½ cup / 85 ml
Onions, chopped	¼ cup / 60 gm
Ginger-garlic (*adrak-lasan*) paste	2 tsp / 12 gm
Turmeric (*haldi*) powder	1 tsp / 2 gm
Coriander (*dhaniya*) powder	1 tsp / 2 gm
Red chilli powder	1 tsp / 2 gm
Cumin (*jeera*) powder	1 tsp / 2 gm
Tomatoes, chopped	50 gm
Salt to taste	
Water	1½ cups / 300 ml

Method

1. Heat the oil in a wok (*kadhai*); add the jackfruit and potatoes and sauté for 10-12 minutes. Keep aside.
2. In the same oil, add the onions, ginger-garlic paste, turmeric powder, coriander powder, red chilli powder and cumin powder. Sauté for 5 minutes.
3. Add the tomatoes and fry till the oil separates.
4. Add the jackfruit, potatoes, salt and water. Cook till the vegetables are tender.
5. Serve hot.

Potato with poppy seeds

Prep. time: 30 min. ● Cooking time: 30 min. ● Serves: 2-4

Ingredients

Potatoes, diced	200 gm
Poppy seeds (*khuskhus*)	50 gm
Mustard (*sarson*) oil	2 tbsp / 20 ml
Turmeric (*haldi*) powder	1 tsp / 2 gm
Salt to taste	
Water	2 cups / 400 ml
Green chillies, chopped	3

Method

1. Boil the poppy seeds in double the quantity of water and grind to a paste. Keep aside.
2. Heat the mustard oil in a wok (*kadhai*); sauté the potatoes for 3-4 minutes.
3. Add the poppy seed paste, turmeric powder, salt and water. Cook till the potatoes are done.
4. Add the green chillies and serve immediately.

Potato and cottage cheese dumplings

Prep. time: 30 min. • Cooking time: 1 hr. • Serves: 6

Ingredients

For the koftas:

Cottage cheese (*paneer*), grated	500 gm
Potatoes, boiled, mashed	3-4
Green coriander (*hara dhaniya*), chopped	3 tbsp / 12 gm
Mixed nuts, finely chopped	3 tbsp / 45 gm
Turmeric (*haldi*) powder	½ tsp / 1 gm
Asafoetida (*hing*) powder	a pinch
Ginger (*adrak*), finely shredded	1 tbsp / 25 gm
Green chillies, deseeded, finely chopped	1-2
Dry mango powder (*amchur*)	½ tsp / 1 gm
Lemon (*nimbu*) juice	1 tsp / 5 ml
Salt	1½ tsp / 6 gm
Cornflour	2 tbsp / 20 gm

Vegetable oil for frying

For the gravy:

Cashew nuts (*kaju*) / almonds (*badaam*) finely chopped	2⅔ tbsp / 45 gm
Ginger (*adrak*), finely chopped	1 tbsp / 24 gm
Green chillies, chopped	2
Coriander (*dhaniya*) powder	1½ tsp / 3 gm
Cumin (*jeera*) powder	1 tsp / 2 gm
Turmeric (*haldi*) powder	½ tsp / 1 gm
Water	1¼ cups / 250 ml
Ghee	5 tbsp / 75 gm
Cumin (*jeera*) seeds	1 tsp / 2 gm
Cinnamon (*dalchini*), 1" stick	1

Cloves (*laung*)	4
Tomatoes, finely chopped	600 gm
Salt to taste	
Green coriander (*hara dhaniya*), chopped	1 tbsp / 4 gm

Method

1. **For the koftas**, knead the cottage cheese till smooth and creamy. Add all the ingredients for the koftas. Knead till the mixture is well mixed.

2. Lightly grease your hands and divide the mixture into 12 portions. Roll each portion into a ball. Place them on a tray lined with plastic wrap.

3. Heat the oil in a wok (*kadhai*); slide in a few balls, at a time, and fry them until golden brown. Remove with a slotted spoon and drain the excess oil on absorbent kitchen towels. Keep aside.

4. **For the gravy**, make a smooth paste of cashew nuts or almonds, ginger, green chillies, coriander powder, cumin powder, turmeric powder and some water.

5. Moderately heat the ghee in a pan; stir-fry the cumin seeds, cinnamon stick and cloves for 10 seconds. Add half the tomatoes and the prepared paste, cook until the mixture is dry and the oil separates. Add the remaining tomatoes, water and salt. Cover the pan and simmer for 10-15 minutes or until the gravy has thickened.

6. Slide in the koftas and bring the gravy to the boil. Spoon the koftas out onto a serving dish. Then pour the gravy over them and garnish with green coriander. Serve hot.

Kashmiri-style cottage cheese with potatoes

Prep. time: 15 min. • Cooking time: 20 min. • Serves: 4-6

Ingredients

Cottage cheese (*paneer*), cut into	
1½" x 2"x ½" pieces	500 gm
Potatoes, peeled, ½"-thick rounds	150 gm
Vegetable oil for frying	1 cup / 170 ml
Water	1½ cups / 300 ml
Turmeric (*haldi*) powder	1 tsp / 2 gm
Ginger powder (*sonth*)	1 tsp / 2 gm
Aniseed (*moti saunf*) powder	2 tsp / 3 gm
Asafoetida (*hing*)	a pinch
Salt to taste	
Black cardamoms (*badi elaichi*), crushed	2
Yoghurt (*dahi*)	3 tbsp / 60 gm
Milk	3 tbsp / 60 ml
Ghee	2 tbsp / 30 gm
Cloves (*laung*), crushed	3
Green cardamoms (*choti elaichi*), crushed	3
Green chillies, sliced	2

Method

1. Heat the oil and fry the cottage cheese until golden at the edges. Immerse them in a pot containing water. Fry the potatoes in the same oil and keep aside.

2. Heat the pot containing the cottage cheese and water over a high flame. Add the turmeric powder, ginger powder, aniseed powder, asafoetida, salt, black cardamoms and potatoes. Cook until the gravy is

reduced to half. Add the yoghurt and milk (whisked together). Bring the mixture to the boil; stirring constantly for 5 minutes; then remove from the flame.

3. In a separate pan, heat the ghee and sauté the cloves and green cardamoms. Add this to the cottage cheese preparation and mix well.

4. Serve hot garnished with green chillies.

Fresh Tricks

Keep the cottage cheese (paneer) fresh for a longer time by immersing it in a bowl of water to which 3 tbsp vinegar has been added.

Cottage cheese in an exotic curry

Prep. time: 30 min. • Cooking time: 20 min. • Serves: 4-5

Ingredients

Cottage cheese (*paneer*), cut into fingers	1 kg
Vegetable oil	5¹/₃ tbsp / 55 ml
Cloves (*laung*)	6
Bay leaves (*tej patta*)	2
Cinnamon (*dalchini*), 1" sticks	3
Green cardamoms (*choti elaichi*)	6
Onion paste	1 cup / 300 gm
Ginger (*adrak*) paste	2²/₃ tbsp / 40 gm
Garlic (*lasan*) paste	2²/₃ tbsp / 40 gm
Red chilli powder	2 tsp / 4 gm
Turmeric (*haldi*) powder	½ tsp / 1 gm
Coriander (*dhaniya*) powder	1 tsp / 2 gm
Cashew nut (*kaju*) paste	2 tsp / 20 gm
Salt to taste	
Red food colouring	a few drops
Yoghurt (*dahi*), whisked	³/₄ cup / 225 gm
Water, warm	½ cup / 100 ml
Sugar	2 tsp / 6 gm
Cream	²/₃ cup / 120 gm
Garam masala (see p. 8)	1²/₃ tsp / 4 gm
Green cardamom (*choti elaichi*) powder	½ tsp / 1 gm
Mace (*javitri*) powder	1 tsp / 3 gm
Vetiver (*kewda*)	3 drops
Saffron (*kesar*), dissolved in 1 tbsp milk	a few strands
Green coriander (*hara dhaniya*), chopped	1 tbsp / 4 gm

Method

1. Heat the oil in a pan; add the cloves, bay leaves, cinnamon sticks and green cardamoms. Sauté over medium heat. When they begin to crackle, add the onion paste and stir-fry for 2-3 minutes.

2. Stir in the ginger and garlic pastes, red chilli powder, turmeric powder, coriander powder, cashew nut paste, salt and red colour.

3. Add the yoghurt, warm water and sugar. Bring the mixture to a slow boil and then simmer until the oil separates.

4. Let the curry cool, remove the whole spices and blend to a smooth consistency.

5. Reheat the curry, stir in the cream, garam masala, cardamom powder, mace powder, vetiver and saffron mixture.

6. Add the cottage cheese and cook further for 5 minutes.

7. Serve hot garnished with green coriander.

Stuffed cottage cheese in tomato curry

Prep. time: 20 min. • Cooking time: 35 min. • Serves: 4

Ingredients

Cottage cheese (*paneer*), cut into 16 finger-sized pieces	600 gm
For the filling:	
Wholemilk fudge (*khoya*)	4 tsp / 25 gm
Cottage cheese (*paneer*), mashed	2 tbsp / 30 gm
Cashew nuts (*kaju*), chopped	2 tsp / 10 gm
Pickle masala (any)	1 tsp / 5 gm
Tomato purée, thick	4 tsp / 20 gm
For the batter:	
Cornflour	3 tbsp / 30 gm
Salt to taste	
Yellow colour	a few drops
Water as required	
For the gravy:	
Vegetable oil	2 tsp / 4 ml + for frying
Ginger-garlic (*adrak-lasan*) paste	2 tsp / 12 gm
Tomato purée, fresh	2½ cups / 500 gm
Salt to taste	
Red chilli powder	½ tsp / 1 gm
White pepper (*safed mirch*) powder	a pinch
Fenugreek (*methi*) powder	a pinch
Garam masala (see p. 8)	2 tsp / 4 gm
Butter	2 tsp / 10 gm
Cream	4 tsp / 24 gm

Method

1. **For the filling,** mix together all the ingredients thoroughly. Stuff this filling between two cottage cheese fingers.
2. **For the batter,** mix together all the ingredients and make a smooth batter. Dip the cottage cheese sandwich in the batter and deep-fry in hot oil for 2-3 minutes. Remove with a slotted spoon and drain the excess oil on absorbent kitchen towels. Keep aside.
3. **For the gravy,** heat the oil in a pan; sauté the ginger-garlic paste for 2-3 minutes. Add the tomato purée and cook for 8-10 minutes until the mixture thickens. Add the seasoning and spices. Cook for 3-5 minutes. Stir in the butter and cream. Mix and remove from heat.
4. Arrange the fried cottage cheese sandwiches on a platter and pour the gravy on top.
5. Serve hot.

Size does Matter!

Small-sized tomatoes contain more vitamins and are tastier than the large ones.

Cottage cheese koftas in spinach curry

Prep. time: 10 min. ● Cooking time: 35 min. ● Serves: 4

Ingredients

For the koftas:

Cottage cheese (*paneer*), mashed	500 gm
Potatoes, boiled, mashed	250 gm
Cornflour	3½ tbsp / 35 gm
Salt to taste	
White pepper (*safed mirch*) powder	½ tsp / 1 gm
Vegetable oil for frying	

For the gravy:

Spinach (*palak*)	1 kg
Vegetable oil	3½ tbsp / 35 ml
Garlic (*lasan*), chopped	1 tsp / 3 gm
Tomato purée	½ cup / 100 ml
Red chilli powder	½ tsp / 1 gm
Turmeric (*haldi*) powder	½ tsp / 1 gm
Coriander (*dhaniya*) powder	½ tsp / 1 gm
Salt to taste	
Water	3 cups / 600 ml
Garam masala (see p. 8)	½ tsp / 1 gm

Method

1. **For the koftas,** mix together all the ingredients. Divide this mixture into 16 even-sized balls.
2. Heat the oil in a wok (*kadhai*); deep-fry the koftas, a few at a time, until golden brown. Remove with a slotted spoon and drain the excess oil on absorbent kitchen towels. Keep aside.

3. **For the gravy,** boil the spinach and when cool, blend to a purée.

4. Heat the oil in a wok; add the garlic, spinach purée and cook for about 2-3 minutes. Stir in the tomato purée and mix well.

5. Add the red chilli powder, turmeric powder, coriander powder and salt. Cook for 4-5 minutes. Pour in the water and bring the mixture to the boil. Stir in the koftas, reduce heat and let the mixture simmer for 5-7 minutes. Stir in the garam masala and cook till the curry has reduced to half. Remove from heat.

6. Carefully remove the koftas with a spoon and place them on a serving dish. Pour the curry on top and serve hot with any Indian bread.

Soft Tip

To make the koftas soft and fluffy, add a pinch of Eno's Fruit Salt to the batter.

Curried spinach balls

Prep. time: 15 min. ● Cooking time: 20 min. ● Serves: 4

Ingredients

For the koftas:

Spinach (*palak*), washed, parboiled	175 gm
Poppy seeds (*khuskhus*)	1 tbsp / 10 gm
Cashew nuts (*kaju*), broken	2 tbsp / 30 gm
Gram flour (*besan*)	1 cup / 100 gm
Coriander (*dhaniya*) powder	½ tsp / 1 gm
Cumin (*jeera*) powder	½ tsp / 1 gm
Red chilli powder	½ tsp / 1 gm
Salt to taste	

Vegetable oil for frying

For the gravy:

Vegetable oil	2 tbsp / 20 ml
Cumin (*jeera*) seeds	½ tsp / 1 gm
Onion, medium-sized, chopped	1
Ginger (*adrak*) paste	1 tsp / 6 gm
Garlic (*lasan*) paste	1 tsp / 6 gm
Cashew nut (*kaju*) paste	2 tbsp / 40 gm
Turmeric (*haldi*) powder	½ tsp / 1 gm
Red chilli powder	1 tsp / 2 gm
Tomatoes, chopped	240 gm
Water	1½ cups / 300 ml
Salt to taste	
Cream	1 tbsp / 20 gm
Green coriander (*hara dhaniya*), chopped	1 tbsp / 4 gm

Method

1. **For the koftas,** parboil the spinach leaves and when cool enough to handle, squeeze out as much water as possible and mash.
2. Grind the poppy seeds and cashew nuts to a paste.
3. Except the oil, mix the remaining ingredients of the koftas with the poppy seed paste and the spinach.
4. Divide this mixture into 8 portions and roll into balls. Heat the oil in a wok (*kadhai*); deep-fry the balls. Remove with a slotted spoon and drain the excess oil on absorbent kitchen towels. Keep aside.
5. **For the gravy,** heat the oil in a wok; add the cumin seeds. When it crackles, add the onions and sauté till brown. Add the ginger and garlic pastes, cashew nut paste, turmeric powder, red chilli powder and salt and fry for 2-3 minutes.
6. Add the tomatoes and fry for another 8-10 minutes. Pour in the water and let the mixture simmer. Check for seasoning.
7. Before serving, add the koftas to the gravy and simmer for a few minutes.
8. Serve hot garnished with cream and green coriander.

Kashmiri kohlrabi curry

Prep. time: 10 min. • Cooking time: 25 min. • Serves: 4-6

Ingredients

Kohlrabi (*ganth gobhi*), with leaves	1 kg
Vegetable oil	3 tbsp / 30 ml
Asafoetida (*hing*)	a pinch
Salt to taste	
Water	1½ cups / 300 ml
Dry red chillies (*sookhi lal mirch*), deseeded	4
Tikki masala, crushed (see p. 8)	½ tsp / 3 gm

Method

1. Separate the leaves of the kohlrabi and cut their stems. Then peel and slice them into wafer-thin pieces. Wash the leaves and slices well and keep aside.
2. Heat the oil in a heavy-bottomed pot; add the kohlrabi, asafoetida and salt. Stir and then add the leaves. Cook for 2 minutes.
3. Add the water and dry red chillies. Cook covered on a high flame for 10 minutes. Stir occasionally. Lower the flame and add the *tikki* masala. Stir well and cook uncovered over a low flame for 5-7 minutes. Traditionally the gravy is thin in consistency, but you can cook to your preference.
4. Serve hot with steamed rice.

Gram flour dumplings in yoghurt curry

Prep. time: 45 min. • Cooking time: 30 min. • Serves: 4

Ingredients

Gram flour (*besan*)	1/2 cup / 50 gm
Yoghurt (*dahi*)	3/4 cups / 135 gm
Salt to taste	
Red chilli powder	1 tsp / 2 gm
Turmeric (*haldi*) powder	1 tsp / 2 gm
Bicarbonate of soda	a pinch
Carom (*ajwain*) seeds	1/2 tsp / 1 gm
Green chillies, chopped	5
Vegetable oil + for frying	4 tbsp / 40 ml
Water	3 cups / 600 ml
Potatoes, cut into rounds	150 gm
Onion, cut in 1/4"-thick rounds	150 gm
Cumin (*jeera*) seeds	1/2 tsp / 1 gm
Mustard seeds (*rai*)	1/4 tsp / 1 gm
Fenugreek seeds (*methi dana*)	1/4 tsp / 1 gm
Dry red chillies (*sookhi lal mirch*)	4
Green coriander (*hara dhaniya*), chopped	1 tbsp / 4 gm

Method

1. Whisk the yoghurt, salt, red chilli powder, turmeric powder and half the gram flour together in a bowl. Keep aside.

2. Sieve the other half of the gram flour and bicarbonate of soda together. Add the carom seeds and enough water to make a thick batter. Add the green chillies and beat well.

3. Heat enough oil in a wok (*kadhai*) to deep-fry. Drop large spoonfuls of the batter to get 1½" puffy dumplings. Fry till golden brown on all sides. Remove with a slotted spoon and drain the excess oil on absorbent kitchen towels. Keep aside.

4. Heat 3 tbsp oil in a pan; add the yoghurt mixture and water. Bring it to the boil, lower heat and simmer for 8-10 minutes, stirring constantly to avoid the yoghurt from curdling. Add the potatoes and onions; cook till the potatoes are tender.

5. Add the dumplings and simmer for 35 minutes. Remove from heat.

6. Heat 1 tbsp oil in a small pan; add the cumin seeds, mustard seeds and fenugreek seeds. Sauté till they crackle. Add the dry red chillies, remove from the fire and pour this tempering over the hot curry.

7. Serve hot garnished with green coriander and accompanied with steamed rice.

Rajasthani-style gram flour dumplings

Prep. time: 30 min. • Cooking time: 40 min. • Serves: 4

Ingredients

Gram flour (besan)	1¼ cups / 125 gm
Ginger (adrak), chopped	3 tsp / 20 gm
Mint (pudina) leaves, chopped	2 tsp / 6 gm
Yoghurt (dahi)	1¼ cups / 225 gm
Vegetable oil for gravy	½ cup / 85 ml
Cumin (jeera) seeds	2 tsp / 4 gm
Red chilli powder	1 tsp / 2 gm
Bicarbonate of soda	a pinch
Vegetable oil for deep-frying	
Coriander (dhaniya) powder	4 tsp / 6 gm
Turmeric (haldi) powder	½ tsp / 1 gm
Salt to taste	
Cloves (laung)	6
Cinnamon (dalchini), 1" stick	2
Bay leaves (tej patta)	2
Asafoetida (hing)	a large pinch
Green coriander (hara dhaniya), chopped	1 tbsp / 4 gm
Garam masala (see p. 8)	¼ tsp / 1 gm
Green chillies, chopped	4

Method

1. Whisk together the ginger, 1 tsp mint leaves with ¼ cup yoghurt.

2. Add ¼ cup oil, gram flour, 1 tsp cumin seeds, half the red chilli powder, bicarbonate of soda and some warm water. Knead into a hard, but pliable dough. Divide the

dough into 8 portions and shape into 6-8"-long cylinders.

3. Boil 6 cups water in a pot; and cook the cylinders for 20 minutes. Remove them with a slotted spoon and keep them and the liquid aside to cool. Cut the cylinders into $1/2$" pieces.

4. Heat the oil in a wok (*kadhai*); deep-fry the cylinders till golden brown.

5. Whisk the remaining yoghurt in a bowl. Add the coriander powder, the remaining red chilli powder, turmeric powder and salt. Keep aside for 10 minutes.

6. Meanwhile, heat 3 tbsp oil. Add the remaining cumin seeds, cloves, cinnamon sticks and bay leaves. When they start crackling, stir in the asafoetida. Reduce the flame and add the yoghurt mixture. Cook on a low flame till the gravy starts boiling. Add 2 cups of the reserved liquid, bring it to the boil and then simmer for 5 minutes.

7. Add the cylinders and simmer for 10 minutes. Remove from the fire.

8. Serve hot garnished with the remaining mint leaves, green chillies and garam masala.

An authentic Rajasthani preparation

Prep. time: 1½ hrs. • Cooking time: 1 hr. • Serves: 2-4

Panchmela Dal
A five-in-one-dal

Ingredients

Black gram (*urad dal*)	¼ cup / 50 gm
Bengal gram (*chana dal*)	¼ cup / 40 gm
Green gram (*moong dal*)	¼ cup / 50 gm
Split red gram (*arhar dal*)	¼ cup / 50 gm
Lentil (*masoor dal*)	¼ cup / 30 gm
Salt to taste	
Turmeric (*haldi*) powder	½ tsp / 1 gm
Water	1¼ cups / 250 ml
Ghee	5 tbsp / 75 gm
Asafoetida (*hing*)	a pinch
Cumin (*jeera*) seeds	½ tsp / 1 gm
Cloves (*laung*)	5
Onions, chopped	2
Ginger-garlic (*adrak-lasan*) paste	2 tbsp / 36 gm
Red chilli powder	1 tsp / 2 gm
Ginger (*adrak*), chopped	2 tsp / 20 gm
Green chillies, chopped	2
Tomatoes, medium-sized, chopped	3
Green coriander (*hara dhaniya*), chopped	1 tbsp / 4 gm
Ginger (*adrak*), julienned	1 tbsp / 24 gm
Green chillies, julienned	4

Method

1. Mix the pulses, wash and soak for half an hour.

2. Cook the pulses with salt, turmeric powder and just enough water until tender.
3. Heat the ghee in a wok (*kadhai*); add the asafoetida, cumin seeds and cloves. Sauté over a medium flame for a few seconds. Add the onions and sauté till golden brown.
4. Add the ginger-garlic paste and red chilli powder. Cook for 3-4 minutes.
5. Add the ginger, green chillies and tomatoes; cook till the mixture leaves the sides of the pan.
6. Add the boiled pulses, mix well and heat thoroughly. Serve hot garnished with green coriander, ginger and green chillies.

Bati
A traditional bread preparation
(makes 14-16 pieces)

Ingredients

Refined flour (*maida*), sieved	2½ cups / 250 gm
Salt to taste	
Ginger (*adrak*) paste	1 tbsp / 18 gm
Garlic (*lasan*) paste	1 tbsp / 18 gm
Green chillies, ground to a paste	3
Ghee	2 cups / 380 gm

Method

1. To the refined flour, add salt, ginger-garlic pastes, green chilli paste and 4 tbsp ghee. Add just enough water to knead into a semi-hard dough.

2. Divide the dough into balls of 2" diameter, to fit the hollow of the palm.
3. Place the balls on a greased tray and bake in a moderately hot oven for 10 minutes. Turn the sides and bake again for 10 minutes. They should be lightly browned with a few cracks when done.
4. Remove and dip in melted ghee. Serve hot.

Choorma
Crumbled bread dessert

Ingredients

Batis (see p. 139) without ginger-garlic	10
Sugar, powdered	1 cup / 150 gm
Ghee	1 cup / 190 gm
Green cardamoms (*choti elaichi*), powdered	8
Almonds (*badaam*), blanched	12

Method

1. Dip the *batis* liberally in melted ghee. Keep aside for 5 minutes to cool.
2. Crush them coarsely; add the sugar, 2 tbsp ghee and the green cardamom powder. Mix well.
3. To serve, either serve as a crushed mixture or roll into round balls which fit in the palm of the hand, garnished with slivers of almonds.

Gram flour cubes in a spicy yoghurt curry

Prep. time: 20 min. • Cooking time: 1 hr. • Serves: 4-6

Ingredients

For the *pithore*:

Gram flour (*besan*)	1¼ cups / 150 gm
Yoghurt (*dahi*)	2½ cups / 750 gm
Ginger-garlic (*adrak-lasan*) paste	2 tbsp / 36 gm
Red chilli powder	1 tsp / 2 gm
Turmeric (*haldi*) powder	½ tsp / 1 gm
Salt to taste	
Green coriander (*hara dhaniya*), chopped	a few sprigs
Ginger (*adrak*), 1" piece, chopped	1
Green chillies, chopped	2
Water	1½ cups / 300 ml
Vegetable oil	¾ cup / 130 ml

For dry *pithore*:

Vegetable oil	3 tbsp / 30 ml
Mustard seeds (*rai*)	1 tsp / 3 gm
Lemon (*nimbu*) juice	1

For gravied *pithore*:

Vegetable oil	½ cup / 100 ml
Cloves (*laung*)	3
Black cardamoms (*badi elaichi*)	2
Cinnamon (*dalchini*) sticks, small	2
Onions, finely chopped	2
Ginger-garlic (*adrak-lasan*) paste	4 tsp / 24 gm
Red chilli powder	1 tsp / 2 gm
Turmeric (*haldi*) powder	½ tsp / 1 gm
Salt to taste	
Coriander (*dhaniya*) powder	2 tbsp / 8 gm

| Yoghurt (*dahi*) | ½ cup / 150 gm |
| Water | 1 cup / 200 ml |

Method

1. **For the *pithore*,** mix together all the ingredients (except the oil) with water.

2. Heat the oil in a wok (*kadhai*). Gradually pour the above mixture and cook till it leaves the sides of the wok.

3. Remove and spread the mixture uniformly on a greased tray. Let it set for 1-2 hours. Cut with a knife into 1" cubes or diamond shapes.

4. **For serving dry *pithore*,** heat the oil in a wok. Add the mustard seeds; when it crackles, add the *pithore* pieces. Stir gently for a minute. Remove from the flame and arrange in a dish.

5. Sprinkle lemon juice on top, garnish with green coriander and serve as a snack.

6. **For serving gravied *pithore*,** heat the oil in a wok. Add the cloves, black cardamoms and cinnamon sticks. Sauté over medium heat for a few seconds. Add the onions and cook till golden brown.

7. Mix the ginger-garlic paste, red chilli powder, turmeric powder, salt and coriander powder with the yoghurt. Add this to the onion mixture. Cook till the oil separates.

8. Add the *pithore* pieces and the water. Bring the mixture to the boil and then simmer for 5 minutes. Serve hot.

Green chilli and aubergine curry

Prep. time: 30 min. • Cooking time: 30 min. • Serves: 4

Ingredients

Green chillies, large, slit	100 gm
Aubergines (*baingan*), small, slit	250 gm
Vegetable oil for frying	
For the gravy:	
Onions, sliced	1/2 cup / 60 gm
Groundnuts (*moongphalli*)	3 tbsp / 45 gm
Sesame (*til*) seeds	5 tsp / 12 gm
Coconut (*nariyal*), dry, grated	6 tbsp / 24 gm
Yoghurt (*dahi*)	2/3 cup / 200 gm
Vegetable oil	1/2 cup / 85 ml
Mustard seeds (*rai*)	1/2 tsp / 1 gm
Fenugreek seeds (*methi dana*)	1/2 tsp / 1 gm
Onion seeds (*kalonji*)	1/2 tsp / 2 gm
Dry red chillies (*sookhi lal mirch*)	5
Curry leaves (*kadhi patta*)	a few
Turmeric (*haldi*) powder	1/2 tsp / 1 gm
Cumin (*jeera*) powder	1/2 tsp / 1 gm
Coriander (*dhaniya*) powder	1/2 tsp / 1 gm
Dry fenugreek (*kasoori methi*) powder	1/2 tsp / 1 gm
Tamarind (*imli*)	3 tbsp / 30 gm
Ginger-garlic (*adrak-lasan*) paste	3 1/2 tbsp / 45 gm

Method

1. Heat the oil in a pan; deep-fry the green chillies and aubergines. Drain the excess oil on absorbent kitchen towels and keep aside.

2. **For the gravy,** deep-fry the onions in the same oil and

keep aside. Broil the groundnuts, sesame seeds and coconut. Blend them with the fried onions and yoghurt to a smooth paste. Keep aside.

3. Heat the oil in a wok (*kadhai*); add the mustard seeds, fenugreek seeds, onions seeds, the prepared paste and the remaining ingredients. Cook till the oil separates.

4. Add the fried green chillies and aubergines. Reduce the heat to low and cook for a few minutes.

5. Remove and serve hot.

Chilli Remedy

If there are too many chillies in any dish, add some tomato sauce or lime juice or sugar, and the dish will lose its pungent taste.

Banana koftas in a thick gravy

Prep. time: 45 min. • Cooking time: 45 min. • Serves: 4

Ingredient

For the koftas:

Raw bananas	450 gm
Onions, finely chopped	1/4 cup / 60 gm
Ginger (*adrak*), finely chopped	1 tbsp / 25 gm
Green coriander (*hara dhaniya*), chopped	4 tsp / 8 gm
Green chillies, chopped	6
White pepper (*safed mirch*) powder	1/2 tsp / 1 gm
Salt to taste	

Vegetable oil for deep-frying	
Green cardamoms (*choti elaichi*)	6
Cloves (*laung*)	4
Cinnamon (*dalchini*), 1" stick	1
Onions, chopped	1/4 cup / 60 gm
Ginger (*adrak*) paste	1 tbsp / 12 gm
Garlic (*lasan*) paste	1 tbsp / 12 gm
Tomatoes, chopped, blended	150 gm
Red chilli powder	1 tsp / 2 gm
Salt	
Water	2 cups / 400 ml
Cream	1/4 cup / 45 gm
Honey	1 tsp / 5 ml
Mace (*javitri*) powder	a pinch
Dough for sealing the dish	

Method

1. **For the koftas,** put the bananas in a pan, cover with water and boil for 30 minutes. Cool, peel and mash.
2. Mix in the onion, ginger, green coriander, green chillies, white pepper powder and salt. Divide the mixture into 15 portions and roll into balls.
3. Heat the oil in a wok (kadhai); deep-fry the balls over low heat till golden brown. Remove with a slotted spoon and drain the excess oil on absorbent kitchen towels. Keep aside.
4. Reheat 4 tbsp oil in the same wok. Add the green cardamoms, cloves and cinnamon stick. When they start crackling, add the onions. Sauté till transparent. Add the ginger and garlic pastes and sauté till the onions turn brown.
5. Add the tomato purée, red chilli powder and salt. Cook till the oil surfaces. Add the water and bring the mixture to the boil. Remove and strain the soup into another pot.
6. Put this pot on fire and bring the gravy to the boil. Add the cream. Remove from heat and add honey.
7. Arrange the koftas in an ovenproof casserole. Pour the gravy over, sprinkle some mace powder, cover and seal the dish with wholewheat dough.
8. Place the dish in a preheated oven at 275°F / 140°C and bake for 8-10 minutes.
9. To serve, open the seal and serve with steamed rice or paratha.

Raw banana curry

Prep. time: 30 min. ● Cooking time: 40 min. ● Serves: 2-4

Ingredients

Raw bananas, diced	50 gm
Potatoes, diced	50 gm
Cauliflower (*phool gobhi*), diced	40 gm
Aubergines (*baingan*), diced	60 gm
Mustard (*sarson*) oil	4 tsp / 20 ml
Panch phoran (see p. 8)	1 tsp / 5 gm
Turmeric (*haldi*) powder	1/2 tsp / 1 gm
Ginger (*adrak*) paste	1 tsp / 6 gm
Salt to taste	
Water	1 1/2 cups / 300 ml

Method

1. Heat the mustard oil in a wok (*kadhai*); add the *panch phoran*. When it crackles, add the potatoes and sauté for a while. Add the raw bananas, cauliflower and aubergines.

2. Add the turmeric powder, ginger paste, salt and water. Cook till the vegetables are soft.

3. Serve hot.

Turnips in a Kashmiri tomato curry

Prep. time: 15 min. • Cooking time: 25 min. • Serves: 6-8

Ingredients

Turnips (*shalgam*), medium-sized, cut into 4 pieces	1 kg
Vegetable oil	3 tbsp / 30 ml
Garlic (*lasan*) paste	1 tsp / 6 gm
Asafoetida (*hing*)	a pinch
Cloves (*laung*)	4
Black cardamoms (*badi elaichi*)	2
Salt to taste	
Tomato purée	1¼ cups / 250 gm
Red chilli powder	½ tbsp / 2 gm
Water	1 cup / 200 ml
Ginger powder (*sonth*)	2 tsp / 4 gm
Aniseed (*moti saunf*) powder	1 tbsp / 3 gm
Tikki masala, crushed (see p. 8)	½ tsp / 3 gm

Method

1. Heat the oil in a wok (*kadhai*); add the garlic paste and asafoetida. Sauté and add the cloves, black cardamoms, salt and turnips. Cook for 5 minutes on a low flame, stirring occasionally.

2. Add the tomato purée and cook till the oil separates. Mix the red chilli powder with a little water and add to the turnip mixture. Mix well till a nice red colour is obtained.

3. Add the water, ginger and aniseed powders. Cook till the turnips become tender. Sprinkle *tikki* masala and cook for 2 minutes. Serve hot.

Tomatoes stuffed with morel mushrooms

Prep. time: 15 min. • Cooking time: 1 hr. • Serves: 4-5

Ingredients

Tomatoes, round and firm	15
Vegetable oil	2 tbsp / 20 ml
Onions, chopped	2 tbsp / 24 gm
Garlic (lasan), chopped	1 tbsp / 12 gm
Green chillies, finely chopped	2
Tomato pulp	100 gm
Morel mushrooms (guchhi), chopped	500 gm
Salt to taste	
Garam masala (see p. 8)	2 tsp / 4 gm
Mint (pudina) leaves, chopped	2 tsp / 6 gm
Lemon (nimbu) juice	2 tsp / 10 ml
Black cumin powder (shah jeera), roasted	1/2 tsp / 1 gm
Green coriander (hara dhaniya), chopped	2 tsp / 4 gm
For the sauce:	
Vegetable oil	2 tbsp / 20 ml
Green cardamom (chhoti elaichi) powder	2/3 tsp / 1 gm
Bay leaf (tej patta)	1
Onion, sliced	4 tsp / 20 gm
Garlic (lasan)	2 tsp / 12 gm
Tomatoes, chopped	300 gm
Water	2 cups / 400 ml
Salt to taste	
Cream	1/3 cup / 60 gm
Mace (javitri) powder	2/3 tsp / 3 gm

Method

1. Slice the top of the tomatoes, keep them aside. Scoop out the pulp from the cups and drain upside down on a paper towel.

2. Heat the oil in a pan; sauté the onions, garlic and tomato pulp over medium heat until the moisture evaporates completely and the oil separates from the mixture.

3. Stir in the green chillies and mushrooms. Cook over high heat for 10-15 minutes or till the mushrooms are soft. Add the salt, garam masala, mint leaves, lemon juice, black cumin powder and 1 tsp green coriander. Mix well. Remove from the fire and set aside to cool.

4. Fill each tomato cup with this mushroom mixture and cover with the tomato top. Bake the stuffed tomatoes in a greased baking tray for 15 minutes.

5. **For the sauce**, heat the oil in a pan. Sauté the green cardamoms, bay leaf, onions, garlic and tomatoes. Then add water and salt; cook for about 30 minutes.

6. Strain the sauce through a fine sieve. Transfer to a saucepan and bring the sauce to a slow boil. Add the cream and mace powder.

7. Pour the sauce over the baked tomatoes and sprinkle the remaining green coriander.

8. Serve hot.

Hyderabadi chilli curry

Prep. time: 15 min. • Cooking time: 35 min. • Serves: 4-5

Ingredients

Green chillies, large, slit lengthwise, deseeded	200 gm
Tamarind (*imli*), soaked in warm water	4 tbsp / 60 gm
Coconut (*nariyal*), grated	1/4 cup / 60 gm
Groundnuts (*moongphalli*)	1/4 cup / 50 gm
Sesame (*til*) seeds	1/4 cup / 30 gm
Coriander (*dhaniya*) seeds, roasted	4 tsp / 8 gm
Cumin (*jeera*) powder	4 tsp / 6 gm
Red chilli powder	2 1/2 tsp / 4 gm
Turmeric (*haldi*) powder	1 tsp / 2 gm
Salt to taste	
Onion paste, browned	1 kg
Ginger (*adrak*) paste	1 tbsp / 12 gm
Garlic (*lasan*) paste	1 tbsp / 12 gm
Vegetable oil	2 1/2 cups / 425 ml
Mustard seeds (*rai*)	1 tsp / 3 gm
Onion seeds (*kalonji*)	1 tsp / 3 gm
Curry leaves (*kadhi patta*)	20
Cumin (*jeera*) seeds	2 tsp / 3 gm

Method

1. Squeeze out the water from the tamarind and retain the pulp.
2. Broil the coconut, groundnuts and sesame seeds. Grind to a fine paste. Mix in the coriander seeds, cumin powder, red chilli powder, turmeric powder, salt, browned onion paste, ginger and garlic pastes.

3. Fill this prepared paste into the slit green chillies. Keep aside.

4. Heat the oil in a wok (*kadhai*); fry the stuffed green chillies to a golden brown. Remove with a slotted spoon and drain the excess oil on absorbent kitchen towels. Keep aside.

5. In the same oil, sauté the mustard seeds, onion seeds, curry leaves and cumin seeds. Stir in the leftover ground paste and the tamarind pulp. Cook on low heat for 10 minutes. Add the fried green chillies and simmer for another 10 minutes.

6. Serve hot.

Greener Greens
Green vegetables will retain their colour if you sprinkle some sugar on them while cooking.

Lotus stems in an exotic curry

Prep. time: 10 min. • Cooking time: 30 min. • Serves: 4

Ingredients

Lotus stems (*kamal kakri*), peeled, cut into 1½" pieces	
discarding the ends, washed	800 gm
Mustard oil	1¼ cups / 220 ml
Water	1 cup / 200 ml
Cloves (*laung*)	2
Green cardamoms (*choti elaichi*)	2
Fennel (*saunf*) powder	2 tbsp / 6 gm
Salt	1 tsp / 4 gm
Cumin (*jeera*) powder	⅓ tsp / 1 gm
Cinnamon (*dalchini*) powder	⅓ tsp / 1 gm
Black cardamom (*badi elaichi*) powder	1 tsp / 2 gm
Yoghurt (*dahi*), whisked	7 cups / 1260 gm

Method

1. Heat the mustard oil in a wok (*kadhai*); deep-fry the lotus stems till half cooked. Remove with a slotted spoon and drain the excess oil on absorbent kitchen towels. Keep aside.
2. In the same wok, add the fried lotus stems and water, bring this to the boil. Add all the spices and mix in the yoghurt. Cook till the curry thickens and the lotus stems are tender, stirring regularly.
3. Serve hot.

Kashmiri radish curry

Prep. time: 10 min. ● Cooking time: 20 min. ● Serves: 4-6

Ingredients

White radish (*safed mooli*), with leaves	1½ kg
Water	2½ cups / 500 ml
Vegetable oil	3 tbsp / 30 ml
Cloves (*laung*)	2
Dry red chillies (*sookhi lal mirch*), deseeded	3-4
Ginger powder (*sonth*)	½ tsp / 1 gm
Salt to taste	
Asafoetida (*hing*)	a pinch
Tikki masala, crushed (see p. 8)	½ tsp / 3 gm

Method

1. Scrape and wash the radish. Remove the ends and dice. Separate the leaves and chop finely.
2. Heat the water in a heavy-bottomed pan. Add the white radish and the leaves. Boil for 10 minutes or until soft. Remove and drain the water. Keep aside to cool.
3. Blend the boiled radish and leaves. Keep aside.
4. Heat the oil in a deep pan; add the cloves and dry red chillies. Stir for a few seconds and then add the radish. Mix well.
5. Reduce the flame and add ginger powder, salt, asafoetida and *tikki* masala. Cook covered for 5 minutes.
6. Serve hot with steamed rice.

Kashmiri kohlrabi stew

Prep. time: 10 min. ● Cooking time: 30 min. ● Serves: 4-6

Ingredients

Kohlrabi (*ganth gobhi*), peeled, cut into 1" cubes	1 kg
Vegetable oil	1¼ cups / 215 ml
Cloves (*laung*)	4
Black cardamoms (*badi elaichi*), crushed	2
Asafoetida (*hing*)	a pinch
Water	1 cup / 200 ml
Turmeric (*haldi*) powder	1 tsp / 2 gm
Ginger powder (*sonth*)	1 tsp / 2 gm
Aniseed (*moti saunf*) powder	1 tbsp / 4 gm
Garam masala (see p. 8)	½ tsp / 1 gm
Salt to taste	
Milk	2 tbsp / 40 ml
Yoghurt (*dahi*)	2 tbsp / 60 gm
Green cardamoms (*choti elaichi*), fried	3

Method

1. Heat the oil in a pan; fry the kohlrabi until golden.
2. Heat 3 tbsp oil in a deep pot; add the cloves, black cardamoms and asafoetida. Sauté, add the water, cover to prevent the oil from spattering. Add the fried kohlrabi, turmeric, ginger, aniseed powders, garam masala and salt. Cook on a high flame for 10 minutes.
3. Add the milk and yoghurt (whisked together), stirring constantly till the mixture comes to the boil. Cook for 5 minutes and then remove. Add the fried green cardamoms and serve hot.

Bengali okra curry

Prep. time: 15 min. • Cooking time: 20 min. • Serves: 2-4

Ingredients

Okra (*bhindi*), washed, dried, slit into halves	200 gm
Mustard (*sarson*) oil	2 tbsp / 30 ml
Mustard paste (see p. 8)	2½ tbsp / 40 gm
Salt to taste	
Green chillies, slit	5
Water	¼ cup / 50 ml

Method

1. Heat the mustard oil in a pan; sauté the okra till half done.
2. Add the mustard paste, salt, green chillies and water.
3. Cook over a medium flame till the okra is soft. Serve hot.

Crunchy Okra

To keep okra crunchy after they are cooked, add salt only when the vegetable is almost done.

A desert speciality

Prep. time: 10 hrs. ● Cooking time: 45 min. ● Serves: 2-4

Ingredients

Sangri (see front cover flap), dried, washed in running water	200 gm
Ker (see front cover flap), dried	50 gm
Yoghurt (*dahi*)	1 cup / 180 gm
Water	2½ cups / 500 ml
Vegetable oil	¾ cup / 130 gm
Onions, medium-sized, chopped	2
Red chilli powder	2 tsp / 4 gm
Coriander (*dhaniya*) powder	3 tbsp / 9 gm
Turmeric (*haldi*) powder	½ tsp / 1 gm
Salt to taste	
Garlic (*lasan*) paste	2 tbsp / 25 gm

Method

1. Soak the *ker* in ½ cup yoghurt and 2 cups water for 10 hours.
2. Pressure cook the *ker* and *sangri* together for 10-15 minutes. Drain the water and transfer them to a wok (*kadhai*). Add all the ingredients (except the garlic paste).
3. Cover and cook on a low flame for 30-45 minutes or till the oil separates.
4. Now add the garlic paste and stir till all the water is absorbed. Add ½ cup warm water and bring the mixture to the boil. Simmer for another 5 minutes. Serve hot.

Baby corn delight

Prep. time: 10 min. • Cooking time: 15 min. • Serves: 4

Ingredients

Baby corn (*bhutta*), boiled, diced into ½" cubes	1½ kg
Ginger-garlic (*adrak-lasan*), ground to paste	4 tsp / 25 gm
Vegetable oil	1 tbsp / 10 ml
Cumin (*jeera*) seeds	½ tsp / 1 gm
Tomato purée	1 cup / 200 ml
Yoghurt (*dahi*), whisked	1 cup / 180 gm
Green peas (*mattar*), shelled	100 gm
Salt	2 tsp / 8 gm
Green coriander (*hara dhaniya*), chopped	1 tbsp / 4 gm

Method

1. Extract the ginger-garlic juice from the paste and discard the pulp.

2. Heat the oil in a wok (*kadhai*); add the cumin seeds and sauté till it starts to crackle. Stir in the tomato purée and cook for about 6-8 minutes or till the raw flavour disappears.

3. Stir in the yoghurt, baby corn and green peas. Cook for about 5 minutes.

4. Season with salt and the ginger-garlic juice. Cook for another 2 minutes or until the gravy thickens.

5. Serve hot garnished with green coriander and accompanied with any Indian bread.

A creamy lentil delicacy

Prep. time: 15 min. ● Cooking time: 30 min. ● Serves: 4

Ingredients

Lentil (*masoor dal*)	1 cup / 110 gm
Water	4 cups / 800 ml
Salt to taste	
Yellow chilli powder	1 tsp / 2 gm
Garlic (*lasan*) paste	1 tbsp / 12 gm
Cream	1/2 cup / 100 gm
Yoghurt (*dahi*)	1 cup / 180 gm
Butter	1/2 cup / 85 gm
Garlic (*lasan*), chopped	1 tbsp / 12 gm
Cumin (*jeera*) seeds	1/2 tsp / 1 gm
Onions, chopped	1/2 cup / 120 gm
Dry red chillies (*sookhi lal mirch*)	4

Method

1. Boil the lentil with water, salt and yellow chilli powder till soft.
2. Add the garlic paste and cook for 10 minutes.
3. Pour in the cream and yoghurt and 1/4 cup butter. Cook again for 10 minutes, stirring frequently so that the fat is incorporated into the lentil mixture.
4. Heat the remaining butter in a pan; add the garlic, cumin seeds and onions; sauté for 2 minutes. Add the dry red chillies and sauté till brown. Pour this mixture into the boiled lentil.
5. Serve hot.

Cottage cheese in spicy tomato purée

Prep. time: 20 min. • Cooking time: 30 min. • Serves: 4

Ingredients

Cottage cheese (*paneer*), cut into 1" cubes	800 gm
Tomatoes, quartered	200 gm
Salt to taste	
Red chilli powder	2 tsp / 4 gm
Ginger (*adrak*) paste	3 tbsp / 54 gm
Garlic (*lasan*) paste	3 tbsp / 54 gm
Butter	1/2 cup / 85 gm
Black cumin (*shah jeera*) seeds	1/4 tsp / 1 gm
Garam masala (see p. 8)	1 tsp / 2 gm
Coriander (*dhaniya*) powder	1 tsp / 2 gm
Mace (*javitri*) powder	a pinch
Processed cheese, grated	1/4 cup / 120 gm
Green coriander (*hara dhaniya*), chopped	2 tsp / 4 gm
Green cardamom (*choti elaichi*) powder	1/2 tsp / 1 gm

Method

1. Boil the tomatoes with little water. Add the salt, red chilli powder, ginger and garlic pastes. Cook for 10 minutes, remove from heat, cool and strain.

2. Melt the butter in a pan. Sauté the cottage cheese. Add the black cumin seeds and when it starts crackling, pour the tomato mixture. Add the garam masala, coriander powder and mace powder. Add the cheese. Bring the mixture to the boil and simmer for 5 minutes on a slow fire.

3. Serve hot garnished with green coriander and cardamom powder.

Spicy lentil curry

Prep. time: 40 min. • Cooking time: 1 hr. • Serves: 4

Ingredients

Split red gram (*arhar dal*), soaked for 30 minutes	200 gm
Water	3½ cups / 700 ml
Coconut (*nariyal*), grated	75 gm
Coriander (*dhaniya*) seeds	1 tsp / 2 gm
Cumin (*jeera*) seeds	2 tsp / 4 gm
Dry red chillies (*sookhi lal mirch*)	2
Groundnut oil	3 tbsp / 30 ml
Mustard seeds (*rai*)	1 tsp / 3 gm
Asafoetida (*hing*)	a pinch
Curry leaves (*kadhi patta*)	15
Green chillies, slit	4
Tamarind (*imli*) pulp, dissolved in 1 cup water	1 tbsp / 6 gm
Drumsticks (*sajan ki phulli*), chopped roughly	200 gm
Turmeric (*haldi*) powder	1 tsp / 2 gm
Red chilli powder	1 tsp / 2 gm
Onions, sliced	1½ cups / 180 gm
Tomatoes, quartered	300 gm
Salt to taste	
Jaggery (*gur*), soaked in 2 tbsp water	10 gm
Green coriander (*hara dhaniya*), chopped	4 tbsp / 20 gm

Method

1. Drain the split red gram and boil with 3 cups water till completely cooked.
2. Prepare the *sambhar* paste, by lightly roasting the coconut, coriander seeds, cumin seeds and dry red chillies. Grind to a paste and keep aside.

3. Heat the oil in a wok (*kadhai*); sauté the mustard seeds and asafoetida till they start to crackle. Add the curry leaves, green chillies, tamarind water, drumsticks, turmeric powder, red chilli powder, onions, tomatoes and salt. Bring the mixture to the boil and simmer for 7-8 minutes.

4. Stir in the prepared paste, the boiled split red gram and the dissolved jaggery. Bring to the boil and simmer for 8-10 minutes.

5. Sprinkle green coriander and serve hot with steamed rice.

Soluble Solution

To thicken watery sambhar add 1 cup of prepared idli batter and bring the mixture to the boil.

Split black gram flavoured with mint

Prep. time: 1 hour. • Cooking time: 45 min. • Serves: 4-6

Ingredients

Split black gram (*urad dal*), soaked for 1 hour	1 cup / 200 gm
Bengal gram (*chana dal*), soaked for 1 hour	½ cup / 80 gm
Salt to taste	
Ginger (*adrak*), chopped	2 tbsp / 36 gm
Garlic (*lasan*), chopped	2 tbsp / 36 gm
Unsalted butter	½ cup / 45 gm
Ghee	½ cup / 95 gm
Onions, chopped	½ cup / 120 gm
Green chillies, chopped	6
Tomatoes, chopped	¼ cup / 50 gm
Mint (*pudina*) leaves	1 tbsp / 4 gm

Method

1. Drain both the grams and cook in 5 cups water in a large pan; add salt. Bring to the boil, reduce heat and keep removing the scum that surfaces.
2. Add 1½ tbsp ginger and garlic each and unsalted butter. Cook covered until the mixed gram is tender and a little water remains. Remove and mash the mixture against the sides of the pan with a large spoon.
3. Heat the ghee in a pan; add the onions and fry until light brown. Add the remaining ginger-garlic, green chillies, tomatoes and mint leaves. Cook until the tomatoes are mashed. Pour this into the above mixture and stir. Serve hot.

Garlic-flavoured split green gram

Prep. time: 15 min. • Cooking time: 30 min. • Serves: 2-4

Ingredients

Split green gram (*moong dal*), washed, soaked for ½ hour	250 gm
Salt to taste	
Turmeric (*haldi*) powder	½ tsp / 1 gm
Ginger (*adrak*), peeled, sliced	½" piece
Green cardamoms (*choti elaichi*)	3
Cloves (*laung*)	4
Ghee	1 tbsp / 15 gm
Asafoetida (*hing*), crushed	a pinch
Cumin (*jeera*) seeds	½ tsp / 1 gm
Garlic (*lasan*), thinly sliced	1 tsp / 3 gm
Jimmu (see front cover flap), optional	½ tsp / 3 gm

Method

1. Heat 5 cups water; add salt, turmeric powder, ginger, green cardamoms and cloves. When the water boils, add the drained split green gram. Cook till done. Remove and keep aside to cool.

2. Remove the ginger, cloves and green cardamoms. Strain the mixture through a thick cloth, pushing with a ladle. The strained mixture should be thick and smooth.

3. Heat the ghee; temper with asafoetida, cumin seeds and garlic. When the garlic turns brown, add the *jimmu*. Pour this mixture over the green gram and serve hot.

Prep. time: 15 min. • Cooking time: 30 min. • Serves: 4-6

Ingredients

Large white gram (*kabuli chana*)	3½ tbsp / 65 gm
Dried peas (*sookhey mattar*)	3½ tbsp / 60 gm
Black-eyed beans (*lobhia*)	3½ tbsp / 65 gm
Dill (*soya beans*) seeds	½ tbsp / 50 gm
White kidney beans (*safed rajma*)	2 tbsp / 50 gm
Whole green gram (*sabut moong*)	2 tbsp / 26 gm
Whole black gram (*sabut urad*)	2 tbsp / 26 gm
Lentil (*masoor dal*)	2 tbsp / 30 gm
Moth beans (*moth*)	4 tsp / 20 gm
Ghee	1 cup / 190 gm
Asafoetida (*hing*)	a pinch
Cloves (*laung*)	5-8
Green cardamoms (*choti elaichi*)	5-6
Cinnamon (*dalchini*), 1" stick	1
Garlic (*lasan*), peeled, crushed	4 tsp / 12 gm
Onions, medium-sized, peeled, finely sliced	2
Turmeric (*haldi*) powder	1 tsp / 2 gm
Salt to taste	
Coriander (*dhaniya*) powder	1 tbsp / 8 gm
Cumin (*jeera*) powder	2 tsp / 4 gm
Black pepper (*kali mirch*) powder	1 tsp / 2 gm
Garam masala (see p. 8)	1 tsp / 2 gm
Red chilli powder	1 tbsp / 5 gm
Yoghurt (*dahi*)	1 cup / 180 gm
Ginger (*adrak*), peeled, ground	4 tsp / 24 gm
Tomatoes, chopped	250 gm
Mustard (*sarson*) oil	¼ cup / 85 ml

Carom (ajwain) seeds	1 tsp / 3 gm
Jimmu (see front cover flap), optional	1 tsp / 5 gm
Dry red chillies (sookhi lal mirch), halved	3-4
Green coriander (hara dhaniya)	1 tbsp / 4 gm

Method

1. Wash and soak the pulses and legumes overnight. Tie them in a muslin cloth and leave for a day to sprout. Repeat the process the next day.

2. Heat the ghee in a pan; add asafoetida, cloves, green cardamoms and cinnamon. Sauté for a while. Add the garlic. When it turns reddish, add the onions and sauté till it turns brown.

3. Add the sprouts, turmeric powder and salt. Fry till the mixture is dry, stirring continuously. Add all the powdered spices, yoghurt and ginger paste. Cook for 5 minutes. Add the tomatoes and 4-5 cups water. Cook till the sprouts become soft. This dish should have a thin gravy, so add more water if required.

4. Heat the mustard oil in a pan till smoking; lower the flame and add carom seeds, jimmu and dry red chillies. Once the dry red chillies turn brown, pour this into the prepared curry and cover the pan with a lid immediately. Remove the lid, garnish with green coriander and lemon wedges. Serve hot.

Broiled green gram

Prep. time: 10 min. • Cooking time: 40 min. • Serves: 2-4

Ingredients

Split green gram (*moong dal*), washed	1 cup / 190 gm
Vegetable oil	2 tbsp / 20 ml
Aniseed (*moti saunf*)	2 tsp / 4 gm
Cloves (*laung*)	3
Green chillies, slit	3
Sugar	1 tsp / 3 gm
Salt to taste	

Method

1. Broil the split green gram on a griddle (*tawa*) till golden brown.
2. Boil 2 cups water in a pot, add the split green gram and cook till done.
3. Heat the oil in a small pan; add aniseed, cloves and green chillies. Sauté just for a few seconds and then add to the split green gram.
4. Add the sugar and salt, stir well and serve immediately.

Bengal gram with coconut

Prep. time: 10 min. • Cooking time: 45 min. • Serves: 2-4

Ingredients

Bengal gram (*chana dal*)	1¼ cups / 200 gm
Turmeric (*haldi*) powder	1 tsp / 2 gm
Vegetable oil	2 tbsp / 20 ml
Aniseed (*moti elaichi*)	1 tsp / 1½ gm
Cinnamon (*dalchini*), 1" stick	1
Coconut (*nariyal*), fresh, cut into thin, small pieces	4 tsp / 8 gm
Salt	1 tsp / 4 gm
Sugar	2 tsp / 6 gm

Method

1. Boil the Bengal gram with turmeric powder and water till soft.
2. Heat the oil in a pan; add the aniseed and cinnamon stick and sauté for a few seconds. Add the coconut and sauté for 5 more minutes.
3. Add the Bengal gram and then cook for 10 minutes.
4. Mix in the salt and sugar. Serve hot.

Narkel Chola Dal

Accompaniments

Unleavened wholewheat bread

Prep. time: 30 min. • Cooking time: 30 min. • Serves: 4-6

Ingredients

Wholewheat flour (*gehu ka atta*), sieved	2 cups / 225 gm
Salt (optional)	½ tsp / 2 gm
Water	¾ cup / 150 ml
Ghee	1 tbsp / 15 gm

Method

1. Mix the wholewheat flour and salt in a bowl. Add the water, knead into a smooth and elastic dough. Cover with a moist cloth and keep aside for 20 minutes at room temperature.
2. Place the dough on a floured board. Divide it into 8 portions, roll out each into a thin disc, the size of a snack plate.
3. Heat a griddle (*tawa*); place one disc on the griddle. Cook until tiny spots appear on one side, flip over and cook the other side for a few seconds. Flip over again and cook till it is pale golden on both sides.
4. Brush lightly with ghee and serve hot with any curry dish.

Spicy gram flour bread

Prep. time: 30 min. • Cooking time: 10 min. • Serves: 4

Ingredients

Gram flour (*besan*)	2¼ cups / 225 gm
Refined flour	½ cup / 50 gm
Green chillies, finely chopped	6-8
Ginger (*adrak*), finely chopped	1 tbsp / 24 gm
Green coriander (*hara dhaniya*), finely chopped	1 cup / 25 gm
Pomegranate (*anardana*) seeds	4 tsp / 12 gm
Cumin (*jeera*) seeds	1 tbsp / 8 gm
Onions seeds (*kalonji*)	5 tsp / 7½ gm
Salt	2 tsp / 8 gm
Water as required	
Ghee	3 tbsp / 45 gm
Butter	5 tbsp / 100 gm

Method

1. Crush the pomegranate seeds, cumin seeds and onion seeds with a rolling pin.
2. Mix the gram flour and flour with the other ingredients except butter and knead with enough water to make a smooth, soft dough.
3. Divide the dough into lemon-sized balls and roll each out into 6"-diameter discs.
4. Cook the discs in a tandoor / griddle (*tawa*) until brown on both sides. Remove, smear butter and serve hot.

Bread cooked on an inverted wok

Prep. time: 1 hr. • Cooking time: 20 min. • Serves: 4

Ingredients

Refined flour (*maida*)	3 cups / 300 gm
Salt	2 tsp / 8 gm
Water	2½ cups / 500 ml
Egg (optional)	1

Method

1. Mix together all the ingredients and knead into a smooth, soft dough. Keep aside for 30 minutes.
2. Divide and shape the dough into lemon-sized balls and keep aside for another 30 minutes. Roll each out into discs and then use your hands to stretch them as thin as possible.
3. Place the disc on an inverted wok (*kadhai*) and cook till tiny brown spots appear on the surface.
4. Remove and serve hot with any dish.

Khameeri Roti

Prep. time: 1 hr. • Cooking time: 30 min. • Serves: 4

Ingredients

Wholewheat flour (*gehu ka atta*)	4 cups / 400 gm
Salt to taste	
Water	1 cup / 200 ml
Yeast, fresh, dissolved in ½ cup warm water	1½ tsp / 7½ gm
Refined flour for dusting	

Method

1. Sieve the wholewheat flour with salt in a bowl. Make a well, pour the water gradually, and knead into a tough dough. Cover with a damp cloth and keep aside for 15 minutes.

2. Slowly sprinkle the dissolved yeast over the dough and keep kneading till the dough is smooth and pliable and not sticky. Cover with a damp cloth and keep aside for 30 minutes.

3. Divide the dough equally into 8 balls and dust with dry flour. Press and flatten each ball into round discs, 8"-wide. Wearing an oven glove stick the disc to one side of a hot tandoor and bake for 2 minutes. Remove with a pair of tongs. Alternately, place on a greased baking tray and bake for 4-5 minutes in a preheated oven at 350°F / 180°C.

4. Serve hot.

Unleavened wholewheat flour bread

Prep. time: 30 min. • Cooking time: 45 min. • Serves: 4

Ingredients

Wholewheat flour (*gehu ka atta*)	4 cups / 400 gm
Salt to taste	
Water	1½ cups / 300 ml

Method

1. Sieve the wholewheat flour and salt together.
2. Make a well in the flour mixture and pour the water. Knead to a soft dough.
3. Cover the dough with a damp cloth and keep aside for 20 minutes.
4. Divide the dough equally into 8 portions. Shape each into balls and dust with flour. Roll out each ball to make 6"-wide discs.
5. Wearing an oven glove, stick the *roti* to one side of a moderately hot tandoor. Bake for 2 minutes then peal off swiftly with a pair of tongs. Alternately, place the *roti* on a greased baking tray and bake for 5-6 minutes at 350ºF / 180ºC in a preheated oven.
6. Serve hot with any curry.

Millet flour unleavened bread

Prep. time: 15 min. • Cooking time: 40 min. • Serves: 4

Ingredients

Millet flour (*bajre ka atta*)	300 gm
Wholewheat flour (*gehu ka atta*)	½ cup / 100 gm
Ghee to smear	

Method

1. Mix the two flours together and knead into a soft dough by adding adequate water.
2. Divide the dough equally into lemon-sized balls. Roll out each ball into flat discs 6-8" in diameter.
3. Heat a griddle (*tawa*) and lay the disc flat on to it. Cook evenly on both sides till golden brown. Remove, smear a little ghee on one side and serve hot. Repeat with the other discs.

Fenugreek-flavoured unleavened bread

Prep. time: 15 min. ● Cooking time: 30 min. ● Serves: 4

Ingredients

Wholewheat flour (gehu ka atta)	4 cups / 400 gm
Fenugreek leaves (methi), finely chopped	1½ cups / 37 gm
Salt to taste	
Red chilli powder	1 tsp / 2 gm
Ghee	½ cup / 95 gm

Method

1. Mix all the ingredients together (except ghee) and knead into a soft dough by adding adequate water.
2. Divide the dough equally into lemon-sized balls and then roll each out into flat discs 6-8" in diameter.
3. Heat a griddle (tawa), lay the disc flat on to it. Bake evenly on both sides till golden brown. Remove, smear a little ghee on one side and serve hot. Repeat with the other discs.

Unleavened bread fried on a griddle

Prep. time: 20 min. • Cooking time: 10 min. • Serves: 4-5

Ingredients

Wholewheat flour (*gehu ka atta*)	5 cups / 500 gm
Salt to taste	
Ghee	1 cup / 190 gm
Water	1½ cups / 300 ml

Method

1. Sieve the wholewheat flour and salt in a bowl, incorporate 2 tbsp ghee, add the water gradually, and knead to a smooth dough.
2. Divide the dough into 5 equal portions and shape each into balls. Dust each with flour, cover with a damp cloth and keep aside for 10 minutes.
3. Flatten each ball and roll out. Brush with ghee and fold over. Brush the folded surface with ghee and fold over again to form a triangle. Roll out the triangle with a rolling pin.
4. Heat a griddle (*tawa*) and brush the surface with ghee. Place the paratha on the griddle and fry for a few minutes. Coat with a little ghee, turn over and fry the other side as well. Both sides of the paratha should be crisp and delicately browned.
5. Remove and serve immediately.

Pudina Paratha

Mint-flavoured unleavened bread

Prep. time: 30 min. • Cooking time: 10 min. • Serves: 4

Ingredients

Wholewheat flour (*gehu ka atta*)	5 cups / 500 gm
Salt	1 tsp / 2 gm
Ghee	¾ cup / 145 gm
Water	1¼ cups / 250 ml
Mint (*pudina*) leaves, dried	1 tbsp / 4 gm

Method

1. Mix the wholewheat flour with salt and half of the ghee. Add the water and knead to a smooth dough. Cover and keep aside for 30 minutes.
2. Shape the dough into a ball, roll out into a big, round disc. Smear the remaining ghee and sprinkle dried mint leaves.
3. Pleat the dough into 1 collected strip. Divide into lemon-sized portions and roll each out into 6"-diameter pancake.
4. Heat a griddle (*tawa*) / tandoor and cook till brown spots appear on both sides.
5. Remove and serve hot.

Cauliflower-stuffed unleavened bread

Prep. time: 45 min. • Cooking time: 45 min. • Serves: 4-5

Ingredients

Wholewheat flour (*gehu ka atta*), sieved	4 cups / 400 gm
Salt	½ tsp / 2 gm
Ghee	1¼ cups / 240 gm
Water, warm	1¼ cups / 250 ml
For the filling:	
Ginger (*adrak*), grated	2 tbsp / 36 gm
Cauliflower (*phool gobhi*), grated	450 gm
Garam masala (see p. 8)	2 tsp / 4 gm
Salt to taste	

Method

1. Mix the wholewheat flour and salt in a bowl. Incorporate ¼ cup ghee. Add water gradually, and knead to a smooth dough. Divide the dough into 20 equal portions and shape each into balls. Cover with a damp cloth. Keep aside for 10 minutes.

2. **For the filling**, heat the remaining ghee in a pan over moderate heat; add the ginger and cauliflower. Sauté until the cauliflower softens. Add the garam masala and salt. Remove from heat. Divide the filling into 10 portions and keep aside.

3. Flatten a ball of dough into a 2" patty. Dust both the sides with flour, roll out into a 6" round. Similarly, roll out the other portions.

4. Spread one portion of the filling evenly over one

round leaving a ½" border around the edges. Place another round on top of the filling. Smooth the surface to ease out any air bubbles, pinch the edges to seal in the filling. Cover and set aside on a lightly floured surface. Similarly, prepare the other portions.

5. Heat a griddle (*tawa*); brush the surface with ghee. Place the stuffed paratha on the griddle and cook for a few seconds, brush with ghee, turn over and similarly fry the other side. Both sides of the paratha should be crisp and delicately browned. Remove and serve immediately.

Note: For variation, substitute cauliflower with mashed potatoes or grated white radish or mashed green peas.

Matter of Weight
Cauliflower and cabbage should be
bought on the basis of their weight.
The heavier the better.

A multi-layered unleavened bread

Prep. time: 1½ hrs. • Cooking time: 45 min. • Serves: 4

Ingredients

Refined flour (*maida*)	4 cups / 400 gm
Salt to taste	
Milk	1 cup / 180 ml
Water	½ cup / 100 ml
Ghee	¾ cup / 145 gm
Fennel (*saunf*) seeds, crushed	2 tsp / 4 gm
Refined flour to dust	
Ghee for shallow frying	

Method

1. Sieve the refined flour and salt. Add the milk and ½ cup water. Knead into a dough. Cover with a moist cloth and keep aside for 10 minutes.

2. Melt ⅓ cup ghee and add to the dough. Knead till a soft and smooth dough is obtained. Add the fennel seeds and knead for 5 more minutes.

3. Divide the dough equally into 12 balls and roll each out into 6" discs. Smear 1 tsp ghee evenly over one side. With a sharp knife, cut from the centre to the outside edge. Roll tightly, from the cut, all the way around so that it makes a neat cone. Stand the cone upright on its base and press it down into a patty. Work the remaining pieces of dough into patties. Refrigerate, covered, for an hour. Roll each out into 6" diameter.

4. Heat a griddle (*tawa*) and shallow fry the paratha on low heat till golden on both sides. Serve hot.

Green cardamom-flavoured leavened bread

Prep. time: 30 min. • Cooking time: 40 min. • Serves: 4

Ingredients

Refined flour (*maida*)	3 cups / 300 gm
Semolina (*suji*)	1 cup / 100 gm
Milk	3 tbsp / 60 ml
Ghee	2 tbsp / 30 gm
Green cardamom (*choti elaichi*) powder	3 tsp / 6 gm
Ginger powder (*sonth*)	2 tsp / 4 gm
Sugar	7 tsp / 20 gm
Salt	2 tsp / 8 gm
Water as required	
Butter	5 tbsp / 100 gm

Method

1. Mix the refined flour, semolina, milk, ghee, green cardamom powder, dry ginger powder, sugar and salt thoroughly.

2. Gradually, add the water and knead into a smooth dough. Divide the dough equally into 8 portions and shape each into balls. Roll out each ball into a 6" diameter.

3. Cook in a tandoor or a griddle (*tawa*) until brown on all sides.

4. Remove from the tandoor or griddle, smear butter and serve hot.

Deep-fried puffed bread

Prep. time: 1-3 hrs. ● Cooking time: 30 min. ● Serves: 5-6

Ingredients

Refined flour (*maida*), sieved	2 cups / 200 gm
Salt	½ tsp / 2 gm
Cayenne pepper or paprika	a pinch
Turmeric (*haldi*) powder	a pinch
Coriander (*dhaniya*) powder	2 tsp / 3 gm
Cumin (*jeera*) powder	1½ tsp / 2½ gm
Vegetable oil	½ tbsp / 5 ml
Water, warm	¾ cup / 150 ml
Vegetable oil for frying	

Method

1. Mix the refined flour, salt, cayenne pepper, turmeric powder, coriander powder and cumin powder. Add oil and rub it in till it is well incorporated. Add water, knead into a medium-soft dough.

2. Lightly grease your palms and knead until the dough is smooth and pliable. Brush with oil and keep aside for 3 hours.

3. Knead again briefly and divide the dough into 16 equal portions; shape each into balls. Compress each into a 2" patty. Dip one end of the patty in oil and roll out into a 5" round; place on a flat surface. Similarly, roll out the other portions.

4. Heat the oil in a wok (*kadhai*); fry one round at a time until it puffs up and is golden brown on both sides. Remove and serve hot.

Sheermal

Delicious rich leavened bread

Prep. time: 1¼ hrs. ● Cooking time: 30 min. ● Serves: 4

Ingredients

Refined flour (*maida*), sieved	4 cups / 400 gm
Salt to taste	
Milk	1¾ cups / 135 ml
Sugar	2 tsp / 6 gm
Vetiver (*kewda*) essence	2 drops
Ghee, melted	1 cup / 190 gm
Saffron (*kesar*), dissolved in 1 tbsp milk	a pinch
White butter for brushing	

Method

1. Heat the milk, add the sugar and stir till it dissolves completely. When cool, add the vetiver essence.
2. Mix the salt with the flour. Add the sweetened milk and knead into a soft dough. Cover with a moist cloth and set aside for 10 minutes.
3. Remove the cloth and knead the dough again, with small amounts of ghee, at a time.
4. Divide the dough equally into 12 balls. Cover and keep aside for 10 minutes. Roll out the balls into 8"-round discs. Prick all over with a fork. Arrange them on a greased baking tray and bake in a preheated oven at 350°F / 180°C for 4 minutes. Remove, brush with saffron and bake again for 4 minutes.
5. Serve immediately smeared with white butter.

Naan

Prep. time: 2½ hrs. • Cooking time: 1 hr • Serves: 4

Ingredients

Refined flour (*maida*)	4 cups / 400 gm
Salt to taste	
Bicarbonate of soda	¼ tsp / 1½ gm
Baking powder	1 tsp / 6 gm
Sugar	2 tsp / 6 gm
Yoghurt (*dahi*)	2 tbsp / 40 gm
Milk	3 tbsp / 60 ml
Water	1 cup / 200 ml
Vegetable oil	2 tbsp / 20 ml
Onion seeds (*kalonji*)	1 tsp / 1½ gm
Melon seeds (*magaz*)	1 tsp / 3 gm
Ghee to grease the tray	
Refined flour to dust	
White butter	2 tbsp / 40 gm

Method

1. Sieve the refined flour, salt, bicarbonate of soda and baking powder.
2. Whisk the sugar, yoghurt and milk together.
3. Make a well in the flour mixture, pour the water and the yoghurt mixture. Mix well. Knead into a smooth dough.
4. Add the oil and knead again so that the oil is absorbed. Cover with a moist cloth and keep aside for 2 hours or till the dough rises.
5. Divide the dough equally into 6 balls. Flatten the balls

and sprinkle onion and melon seeds. Cover and set aside for 5 minutes.

6. Flatten each ball between your palms and roll out. Stretch the rolled out dough to one side to give the *naan* an oval shape.

7. Using oven gloves or a cushion pad, stick the *naan* inside a moderately hot tandoor for 3 minutes. Alternately, place the *naan* on a greased tray and bake in an oven for 10 minutes at 375°F / 190°C.

8. Serve immediately smeared with butter, if desired.

Minimum Wastage

Don't discard the whey after making cottage cheese. Knead the chapati or poori dough with it. They will turn out softer and tastier.

Kandhari Pulao

Prep. time: 40 min. • Cooking time: 1 hr. • Serves: 4

Ingredients

Rice, Basmati, soaked for 30 minutes, drained	300 gm
Ghee	1 cup / 190 gm
Garam masala, whole	10 gm
Water	2¼ cups / 450 ml
Saffron (kesar), soaked in ½ cup warm milk	a few strands
Cashew nuts (kaju), broken, fried	½ cup / 60 gm
Walnuts (akhrot), fried	½ cup / 60 gm
Almonds (badam), fried	½ cup / 60 gm
Groundnuts (moongphalli), fried	½ cup / 60 gm
Pistachios (pista), fried	½ cup / 60 gm
Raisins (kishmish), fried	6 tbsp / 60 gm
Rose water (gulab jal)	1 tbsp / 15 ml
Onions, fried	½ cup / 120 gm

Method

1. Heat the ghee in a pan; add the whole garam masala. Sauté till they crackle. Add the rice and fry till a pleasing smell emanates. Add water and boil till the rice is ¾th done. Drain.
2. Mix all the dry fruits together.
3. In a pot, sprinkle some saffron mixture, spread a layer of rice and dry fruits, then the remaining saffron mixture, rose water and fried onions. Seal the pot with aluminium foil.
4. Cook on very low heat for 30 minutes. Remove from heat and serve hot.

Peas pulao

Prep. time: 25 min. ● Cooking time: 30 min. ● Serves: 4-5

Ingredients

Rice, Basmati, soaked for 10 minutes	2 cups / 400 gm
Green peas (*mattar*), boiled	200 gm
Vegetable oil	2 tsp / 4 ml
Cumin (*jeera*) seeds	2 tsp / 4 gm
Salt to taste	
Water	4 cups / 800 ml

Method

1. Heat the oil in a heavy-bottomed pan; sauté the cumin seeds till it crackles.
2. Add the boiled green peas and salt. Stir-fry for a few minutes and keep aside.
3. In a separate pan, add the water and bring it to the boil. Stir in the rice and cook till done. Drain the excess water.
4. Gently mix the green peas with the rice and serve hot with any curry dish.

Broccoli and carrot pulao

Prep. time: 2½ hrs. • Cooking time: 30 min. • Serves: 4

Ingredients

Rice, Basmati, soaked for 10 minutes	2 cups / 400 gm
Broccoli, cut into small florets	150 gm
Carrots (gajar), diced, parboiled	100 gm
Vegetable oil	2 tbsp / 20 ml
Cumin (jeera) seeds	1½ tsp / 3 gm
Bay leaf (tej patta)	1
Cloves (laung)	3
Black peppercorns (sabut kali mirch)	1 tsp / 2 gm
Salt to taste	
Water	6 cups / 1200 ml

Method

1. Heat the oil in a heavy-bottomed pan; add the cumin seeds, bay leaf, cloves, and black peppercorns. When they start crackling, add the carrots, broccoli and salt. Stir-fry for 3-4 minutes.
2. Remove and discard the whole spices and keep the vegetables aside.
3. In a separate pot, bring the water to the boil, add the rice and cook until done. Drain the excess water.
4. Gently mix the cooked vegetables with the rice and serve hot with any curry dish.

A delightful blend of rice with jackfruit

Prep. time: 45 min. ● Cooking time: 30 min. ● Serves: 4-5

Ingredients

Rice, Basmati or any long-grain variety, soaked for 30 minutes	1 cup / 200 gm
Jackfruit (*kathal*), cleaned, cubed	250 gm
Vegetable oil	1 cup / 170 ml
Cloves (*laung*)	4
Cinnamon (*dalchini*), ½" stick	1
Bay leaf (*tej patta*)	1
Black cardamoms (*badi elaichi*)	2
Black cumin (*shah jeera*) seeds	1 tsp / 2 gm
Onions, chopped	¼ cup / 60 gm
Ginger (*adrak*) paste	2 tsp / 12 gm
Red chilli powder	½ tsp / 1 gm
White pepper (*safed mirch*) powder	½ tsp / 1 gm
Salt to taste	
Water	2½ cups / 500 ml
For the garnishing:	
Ginger (*adrak*), julienned	½ tsp / 3 gm
Green chillies, sliced, deseeded	3
Onion, sliced, fried	1
Mace (*javitri*) powder	½ tsp / 1 gm
Lemon (*nimbu*) juice	1 tbsp / 15 ml
Cashew nuts (*kaju*), sliced, fried	1 tsp / 5 gm
Green coriander (*hara dhaniya*), chopped	½ tbsp / 2 gm
Cream	2 tbsp / 40 gm

Method

1. Heat the oil in a wok (*kadhai*) or a pan till smoking. Fry the jackfruit till light brown. Remove and drain the excess oil on absorbent kitchen towels. Keep aside.
2. Reheat the same oil, add the cloves, cinnamon stick, bay leaf, black cardamoms and cumin seeds. Sauté over medium heat until they begin to crackle.
3. Add the onions and sauté. Stir in the ginger paste and red chilli powder. Add the fried jackfruit, white pepper and salt. Cook for 3-4 minutes.
4. Pour in the water. Add the drained rice to the pan and bring the mixture to the boil. Then lower heat and cover the pan. Cook on low heat till the rice is done.
5. Remove the lid and sprinkle ginger, green chillies, fried onion, mace powder, lemon juice, fried cashew nuts, green coriander and cream.
6. Seal the lid with a dough and cook on very low heat for 10-15 minutes.
7. Serve hot with any *raita*.

Note: For vegetable pulao substitute jackfruit with any mixed vegetable and follow the same method.

Nepalese black-eyed bean pulao

Prep. time: 4-5 hrs. • Cooking time: 1 hr. • Serves: 2-4

Ingredients

Rice, soaked for 1 hour	1¼ cups / 250 gm
Black-eyed beans (*lobhia*), soaked for 4-5 hours or overnight	1 cup / 150 gm
Onions, medium-sized, thinly sliced	2
Fenugreek seeds (*methi dana*)	½ tsp / 1½ gm
Garlic (*lasan*), peeled, ground	1 tsp / 6 gm
Ginger (*adrak*), scraped, ground	1 tsp / 6 gm
Turmeric (*haldi*) powder	½ tsp / 1 gm
Cumin (*jeera*) seeds, ground	1 tsp / 1 gm
Red chilli powder	1 tsp / 2 gm
Coriander (*dhaniya*) seeds, ground	1 tsp / 2 gm
Tomatoes, chopped	150 gm
Water	5 cups / 1 lt
Garam masala (see p. 8)	1 tsp / 2 gm
Vegetable oil	3 tbsp / 30 gm
Ghee	2 tbsp / 30 gm
Green cardamoms (*choti elaichi*)	2
Cloves (*laung*)	4

Method

1. Heat the oil in a pressure cooker and fry the onions till brown. Remove with a slotted spoon and keep aside.
2. In the same oil, add the fenugreek seeds, ground garlic and ginger. Fry for 10 minutes. Add the turmeric powder, cumin powder, red chilli powder, coriander powder and tomatoes. Cook till the oil separates.

3. Add the drained black-eyed beans and salt. Fry for a while. Add the water and pressure cook for 5 minutes. Remove from the fire and keep aside. Check whether the beans are cooked or not. If not, cook further for a while.

4. Heat the ghee in a heavy-bottomed pan, add the green cardamoms and cloves. When they stop crackling, add the drained rice. Fry for 4-5 minutes, stirring gently so that the rice does not break.

5. Add the beans and water, and bring the mixture to the boil. Add the garam masala and half the fried onions. Cook covered over a low flame stirring once, very gently, till the water dries completely. Then cook covered till done.

6. Just before serving stir once gently and serve with the remaining fried onions.

Garlic Wormicide

To protect rice from worms, place a few garlic flakes in the container.

Rajasthani fried rice with green gram dumplings

Prep. time: 15 min. • Cooking time: 25 min. • Serves: 4-6

Ingredients

Rice, Basmati, soaked for 10 minutes	3 cups / 600 gm
Mangodi (see front cover flap)	200 gm
Vegetable oil	1 cup / 170 ml
Green cardamoms (*choti elaichi*)	5
Black cardamoms (*badi elaichi*)	2
Cloves (*laung*)	5
Cinnamon (*dalchini*), 1" sticks	2
Bay leaves (*tej patta*)	2
Cumin (*jeera*) seeds	½ tsp / 1 gm
Salt to taste	
Water	7 cups / 1½ lt
Onion, sliced, browned	1

Method

1. Heat 2 tbsp oil in a wok (*kadhai*); shallow fry the *mangodis* on a medium flame for 2-3 minutes.

2. Heat the remaining oil in a pan; add the green and black cardamoms, cloves, cinnamon sticks, bay leaves and cumin seeds. Sauté over a medium flame till they crackle. Add the drained rice and *mangodis*. Stir gently.

3. Add the salt and water. Bring the mixture to the boil, lower the flame and cook until the liquid dries, stirring occasionally and gently.

4. Serve hot garnished with browned onion.

Bengali soft cottage cheese pilaf

Prep. time: 20 min. • Cooking time: 10 min. • Serves: 2-4

Ingredients

Rice, Basmati, soaked for 2 hours	1¼ cups / 250 gm
Soft cottage cheese (*paneer*)	50 gm
Ghee	2 tbsp / 30 gm
Cloves (*laung*)	2
Green cardamoms (*choti elaichi*)	2
Cinnamon (*dalchini*), 1" stick	1
Bay leaf (*tej patta*)	1
Saffron (*kesar*), soaked in 2 tsp milk	a pinch
Salt to taste	
Water, hot	3 cups / 600 ml

Method

1. Drain the rice and spread it out on a tray to dry.
2. Heat the ghee in a wok (*kadhai*); add the cloves, green cardamoms, cinnamon stick, bay leaf and soft cottage cheese.
3. Cook till the cottage cheese is slightly golden brown.
4. Add the rice, saffron soaked in milk, salt and water. Cook covered on a medium flame, till the rice is done and the water is absorbed.
5. Serve hot.

Kashmiri mixed vegetable rice

Prep. time: 15 min. ● Cooking time: 30 min. ● Serves: 2-4

Ingredients

Rice, cleaned, washed	1½ cups / 300 gm
Ghee	4 tbsp / 60 gm
Cloves (laung)	4
Black cardamoms (badi elaichi), crushed	2
Cauliflower (phool gobhi), cut into florets	500 gm
Potatoes, peeled, cut into 4 pieces	250 gm
Green peas (mattar), shelled	250 gm
Asafoetida (hing)	a pinch
Salt to taste	
Turmeric (haldi) powder	1 tsp / 2 gm
Water	3 cups / 600 ml
Ginger powder (sonth)	1 tsp / 2 gm
Green chillies, slit	2
Ginger (adrak), fresh, ½" piece, julienned	1

Method

1. Heat the oil in a heavy-bottomed pot; add the cloves and black cardamoms, stir. Add all the vegetables, asafoetida, salt and turmeric powder. Stir for 1 minute.

2. Add the rice, water, ginger powder, green chillies and ginger. Cook covered for 20 minutes, stirring occasionally.

3. When the water is almost absorbed, transfer the pot over a griddle. Cook covered over a low flame for 5-7 minutes or until the rice is done. Serve with yoghurt or pickle.

Nepalese fried rice

Prep. time: 20 min. • Cooking time: 45 min. • Serves: 2-4

Ingredients

Rice	1¼ cups / 250 gm
Split black gram (*urad dal*)	100 gm
Ginger (*adrak*), scraped, sliced	2 tsp / 20 gm
Salt to taste	
Ghee	4 tsp / 16 gm
Asafoetida (*hing*)	a pinch
Cumin (*jeera*) seeds	1 tsp./ 2 gm
Dry red chillies (*sookhi lal mirch*), halved	2-3
Garlic (*lasan*), peeled, chopped	1 tsp / 3 gm
Onions, peeled, thinly sliced	2

Method

1. Boil the rice, ensuring that the grains remain separated.
2. Boil the split black gram in an iron utensil with ginger, salt and 1½ cups water till the mixture is dry, but not overcooked.
3. Heat the ghee in a heavy-bottomed pan; add the asafoetida, cumin seeds and dry red chillies. Fry over low heat till brown.
4. Add the garlic, sauté till it turns light brown. Add the onions and fry till brown.
5. Add the rice and split black gram. Cook over a low flame till the liquid gets absorbed.
6. Serve hot with yoghurt.

Vegetable biryani

Prep. time: 45 min. • Cooking time: 30 min. • Serves: 4-5

Ingredients

Rice, Basmati or any long-grain variety, soaked for 30 minutes	1 cup / 200 gm
Carrots (*gajar*), diced, parboiled	20 gm
Cauliflower (*phool gobhi*), cut into small florets	20 gm
Green peas (*mattar*), parboiled	20 gm
Morel mushrooms (*guchhi*), quartered	20 gm
Vegetable oil	4 tbsp / 40 ml
Cloves (*laung*)	4
Cinnamon (*dalchini*), 1" stick	1
Bay leaf (*tej patta*)	1
Green cardamoms (*choti elaichi*)	3
Black cumin (*shah jeera*) seeds	1 tsp / 2 gm
Onions, chopped	¼ cup / 60 gm
Ginger (*adrak*) paste	2 tsp / 12 gm
Red chilli powder	½ tsp / 1 gm
White pepper powder (*safed mirch*)	½ tsp / 1 gm
Salt to taste	
Water	2½ cups / 500 ml

For the garnishing:

Green chillies, slit	3-4
Onions, sliced, fried	1
Mace (*javitri*) powder	½ tsp / 2 gm
Lemon (*nimbu*) juice	1 tbsp / 15 ml
Ginger (*adrak*), julienned	1 tsp / 3 gm
Cashew nuts (*kaju*), fried till golden	10
Green coriander (*hara dhaniya*), chopped	1 tbsp / 4 gm
Cream	2 tbsp / 40 gm

Method

1. Heat the oil in a heavy-bottomed pan; sauté the cloves, cinnamon stick, bay leaf, green cardamoms and black cumin seeds till they begin to crackle.
2. Add the onions, stir-fry till transparent. Stir in the ginger paste, red chilli powder, all the vegetables, white pepper powder and salt. Cook for 3-4 minutes.
3. Stir in the drained rice and water. Bring the mixture to the boil, then lower heat and cook covered till the rice is almost done.
4. Remove the lid and sprinkle green chillies, onions, mace powder, lemon juice, ginger, cashew nuts, green coriander and cream.
5. Seal the lid with a dough, and cook on very low heat for 10-15 minutes.
6. Serve hot with yoghurt.

Farm Fresh

Stale carrots will taste fresh if soaked in cold water, overnight.

A delightful blend of rice and pulses

Prep. time: 1 hr. • Cooking time: 45 min. • Serves: 4

Ingredients

Bengal gram (*chana dal*)	1 tbsp / 25 gm
Kidney beans (*rajma*)	1 tbsp / 25 gm
Split red gram (*arhar dal*)	1 tbsp / 25 gm
Split green gram (*moong dal*)	1 tbsp / 20 gm
Rice	¾ cup / 150 gm

Ground to a paste:

Coriander (*dhaniya*) powder	2 tsp / 3 gm
Cumin (*jeera*) powder	1 tsp / 1½ gm
Coconut (*nariyal*), grated	¾ cup / 180 gm
Red chilli powder	1 tsp / 2 gm

Vegetable oil	3½ tbsp / 35 ml
Cinnamon (*dalchini*), 1" sticks	3
Cloves (*laung*)	6
Bay leaves (*tej patta*)	2
Green cardamoms (*choti elaichi*)	15
Garlic (*lasan*), chopped	1⅓ tsp / 4 gm
Tomatoes, skinned, deseeded	120 gm
Salt to taste	
Water	2½ cups / 500 ml
Almonds (*badam*), blanched, fried	¼ cup / 50 gm
Mint (*pudina*) leaves, chopped	2 tsp / 8 gm
Onion rings, fried	¼ cup / 60 gm

Method

1. Soak the Bengal gram, kidney beans and red gram together for 1 hour. Soak the rice and split green gram together in a separate container for 1 hour.

2. Drain the water from both the containers. Add ¾ cup fresh water to the pot with Bengal gram and cook over medium heat until tender.

3. Add 1½ cups fresh water to the pot with rice and cook on medium heat until almost done.

4. **For the paste,** grind the spices in a food processor with a little water.

5. Heat the oil in a pan; add the cinnamon sticks, cloves, bay leaves and green cardamoms. Sauté for 30 seconds. Add the garlic, tomatoes and the ground paste. Cook for 4-5 minutes or till the oil separates.

6. Add the pulses, rice mixture, salt and water. Cover and cook on low heat till done.

7. Serve hot garnished with almonds, mint leaves and onion rings.

Perky Pulao

*One or two soup cubes added to
any pulao enhance the taste.*

Lemon rice

Prep. time: 5 min. • Cooking time: 25 min. • Serves: 4

Ingredients

Rice, Basmati or any long-grain variety, soaked for 10 minutes, drained	½ cup / 100 gm
Lemon (nimbu) juice	⅓ cup / 80 ml
Water	1 cup / 200 ml
Salt	1 tsp / 4 gm
Vegetable oil	3 tbsp / 30 ml
Cashew nuts (kaju), chopped, fried	½ cup / 60 gm
Lentil (masoor dal)	½ tbsp / 7½ gm
Mustard seeds (rai)	1 tsp / 3 gm
Dry red chillies (sookhi lal mirch)	2-3
Turmeric (haldi) powder	½ tsp / 1 gm
Green coriander (hara dhaniya), chopped	3 tsp / 12 gm
Coconut (nariyal), fresh, grated	¼ cup / 60 gm

Method

1. Boil the water, add the rice, salt and ½ tbsp oil. Cook, covered tightly, on low heat, without stirring until the rice is fluffy and tender and the water is fully absorbed. Keep aside. Sprinkle the cashew nuts over the rice.

2. Heat the oil, sauté the lentil and mustard seeds till the lentil turns reddish brown and the mustard seeds start spluttering. Add the dry red chillies, mix well. Remove and add to the cooked rice along with the turmeric powder, lemon juice, green coriander and coconut. Mix gently with a fork. Serve hot with yoghurt.

Prep. time: 6-8 hrs. • Serves: 4

Ingredients

Milk	5½ cups / 1 lt
Yoghurt (*dahi*), for fermentation	1 tsp / 10 gm

Method

1. Boil the milk in a pan and keep aside till lukewarm.
2. Add the starter yoghurt to the milk and mix well. Keep aside to set in a warm place for 6-8 hours.
3. Once set, refrigerate to chill. Serve cold as an accompaniment with any meal

Prevention is Better than Cure

To prevent the yoghurt from turning sour, add a piece of coconut to it.

Spiced yoghurt

Prep. time: 15 min. • Serves: 4

Ingredients

Yoghurt (*dahi*), whisked	2½ cups / 440 gm
Garlic (*lasan*), crushed	2 tsp / 5 gm
Salt to taste	
Yellow chilli powder	½ tsp / 1 gm
Cumin (*jeera*) powder	½ tsp / 1 gm

Method

1. Mix the garlic with salt. Add to the whisked yoghurt.
2. Reserve a bit of the yellow chilli powder and cumin powder and mix the rest in the yoghurt.
3. Pour into a serving bowl. Sprinkle the reserved powders in a decorative design on the yoghurt.
4. Serve chilled accompanied with biryani.

Mixed vegetables in yoghurt

Prep. time: 30 min. • Serves: 4

Ingredients

Yoghurt (*dahi*)	2½ cups / 440 gm
Cumin (*jeera*) seeds	1 tsp / 2 gm
Coriander (*dhaniya*) seeds	1 tsp / 2 gm
Black peppercorns (*sabut kali mirch*)	½ tsp / 1 gm
Salt to taste	
Cucumber, medium-sized, chopped	½
Green chillies, finely chopped	2
Mint (*pudina*) leaves, finely chopped	1 tsp / 2 gm
Onions, chopped	3 tbsp / 36 gm
Tomatoes, chopped	30 gm
Red chilli powder	a pinch

Method

1. Heat a griddle (*tawa*) and broil the cumin seeds, coriander seeds and black peppercorns till dark and aromatic. Pound and keep aside.
2. Whisk the yoghurt with salt. Add all the vegetables.
3. Pour into a glazed earthenware bowl. Sprinkle some red chilli powder and the pounded spices.
4. Serve chilled.

Note: 60 gm squeezed pineapple chunks can also be added for variation.

Fried okra in yoghurt

Prep. time: 15 min. • Cooking time: 15 min. • Serves: 4

Ingredients

Okra (*bhindi*), washed, dried, sliced diagonally into 2 mm-thick pieces	100 gm
Vegetable oil for frying	
Yoghurt (*dahi*), thick	4½ cups / 810 gm
Salt to taste	
Red chilli powder	a pinch
Cumin (*jeera*) seeds, roasted, powdered	a pinch

Method

1. Heat the oil in a wok (*kadhai*); deep-fry the okra till crisp. Remove and drain the excess oil on absorbent kitchen towels.
2. Whisk the yoghurt with salt. Add the fried okra and mix well.
3. Garnish with red chilli powder and cumin powder. Serve chilled.

Crisp gram flour granules in yoghurt

Prep. time: 10 min. • Cooking time: 20 min. • Serves: 4

Ingredients

Gram flour (*besan*)	2½ tbsp / 25 gm
Salt	¼ tsp / 1 gm
Baking powder	½ tsp / 2 gm
Water as required	
Vegetable oil for frying	
Yoghurt (*dahi*), thick	4½ cups / 810 gm
Cumin (*jeera*) seeds, roasted, crushed	a pinch
Red chilli powder	½ tsp / 1 gm

Method

1. Mix the gram flour, salt and baking powder in a bowl. Whisk into a smooth batter with a little water.
2. Heat the oil in a pan; pour about 2 tbsp batter, at a time, through a slotted spoon to form small granules. These will froth in the hot oil, then rise to the surface. Fry until crisp and golden. Remove and drain the excess oil. Repeat till all the batter is used up.
3. Transfer the gram flour granules in a bowl containing warm water. When the granules turn soft, squeeze the excess water. Keep aside.
4. Whisk the yoghurt with salt, cumin seeds, red chilli powder in a bowl until smooth and creamy.
5. Add the gram flour granules and serve at room temperature or chilled.

Whisked yoghurt with raisins and honey

Prep. time: 15 min. • Serves: 4

Ingredients

Yoghurt (*dahi*), whisked	4 cups / 720 gm
Honey	5 tbsp
Raisins (*kishmish*), chopped	2 tbsp / 20 gm
Cucumber (*khira*), peeled, finely chopped	450 gm
White pepper (*safed* mirch) powder	½ tsp / 1 gm
Salt to taste	
Cumin (*jeera*) seeds, roasted, powdered	½ tsp / 1 gm
Green coriander (*hara dhaniya*), chopped	1 tbsp / 4 gm

Method

1. To the whisked yoghurt add honey, raisins, cucumber, white pepper powder and salt. Mix well. Transfer the mixture to a serving bowl.
2. Sprinkle cumin powder and garnish with green coriander.
3. Serve chilled or at room temperature with any meal.

Prep. time: 15 min. ● Serves: 4

Ingredients

Yoghurt (*dahi*), thick	4½ cups / 810 gm
Salt to taste	
Oranges, peeled, separated into segments, cut into 10 mm cubes	200 gm
Cumin (*jeera*) seeds, roasted, pounded	a pinch

Method

1. Whisk the yoghurt and salt together.
2. Add the oranges and mix well.
3. Serve chilled garnished with cumin powder.

Perfect Setting

For tasty and perfectly set yoghurt, rub the inside of the vessel meant for setting yoghurt with a piece of alum.

Yoghurt flavoured with fried onions

Prep. time: 15 min. • Cooking time: 15 min. • Serves: 4-6

Ingredients

Yoghurt (*dahi*), whisked	2½ cups / 440 gm
Water	½ cup / 100 ml
Salt	1 tsp / 4 gm
Vegetable oil	1 tbsp / 10 ml
Cumin (*jeera*) seeds	1 tsp / 2 gm
Onions, small, chopped	2
Red chilli powder	½ tsp / 1 gm
Turmeric (*haldi*) powder	¼ tsp / 1 gm

Method

1. Mix the yoghurt, water and salt together; keep aside.
2. Heat the oil in a wok (*kadhai*); add the cumin seeds and when it crackles, add the onions and fry till brown. Add the red chilli powder and turmeric powder. Mix and remove from the flame.
3. Pour this mixture into the yoghurt mixture and mix well.
4. Smoke the *raita* with ghee.

Chutneys and Pickles

Fig chutney

Prep. time: 20 min. • Cooking time: 20 min. • Serves: 4

Ingredients

Figs (*anjeer*), dried, blanched for 10 minutes	500 gm
Almond (*badam*), blanched for 10 minutes	4 tbsp / 60 gm
Vegetable oil	½ cup / 85 ml
Onions, chopped	⅓ cup / 100 gm
Garlic (*lasan*), chopped	¾ cup / 100 gm
Sugar	1 tbsp / 20 gm
Red chilli powder	1 tsp / 2 gm
Green chillies, chopped	4-5
Salt to taste	
Malt vinegar	3½ tbsp / 50 ml
White vinegar	5 tsp / 25 ml
Green cardamom (*choti elaichi*) powder	2 tsp / 4 gm
Melon (*magaz*) seeds	2 tsp / 6 gm

Method

1. Heat the oil in a pan; fry the onions and garlic until golden brown. Remove and keep aside.
2. Combine all the ingredients (except the green cardamom powder and melon seeds) and blend to a fine paste.
3. Transfer the paste into a bowl and garnish with green cardamom powder and melon seeds.
4. Refrigerate and use as required. (This can be refrigerated in an airtight container for 1-2 months).

Sesame seeds and tomato chutney

Prep. time: 15 min. • Cooking time: 20 min. • Serves: 4

Ingredients

Tomatoes, chopped	200 gm
Sesame (*til*) seeds	2 tbsp / 15 gm
Vegetable oil	2 tbsp / 20 ml
Onions, chopped	¾ cup / 150 gm
Red chilli powder	½ tsp / 1 gm
Turmeric (*haldi*) powder	½ tsp / 1 gm
Asafoetida (*hing*) powder	a pinch
Split black gram (*urad dal*), roasted	20 gm
For the tempering:	
Vegetable oil	2 tbsp / 20 ml
Dry red chillies (*sookhi lal mirch*)	5
Curry leaves (*kadhi patta*)	a few
Mustard (*rai*) seeds	½ tsp / 1½ gm

Method

1. Heat the oil in a pan; add the onions and sauté till light brown. Add the red chilli powder, turmeric powder, asafoetida and sesame seeds. Sauté for a few minutes.
2. Add the tomatoes and split black gram. Cook for 10 minutes. Remove from heat and keep aside to cool. Blend to a fine paste.
3. **For the tempering**, heat the oil in a pan; add the dry red chillies, curry leaves and mustard seeds. Sauté till they crackle. Remove from heat, mix into the prepared chutney and serve.

Til aur Tamatar Chutney

Mint chutney

Prep. time: 20 min. • Serves: **4**

Ingredients

Mint (*pudina*) leaves, chopped	4 cups / 100 gm
Green coriander (*hara dhaniya*), chopped	4 cups / 100 gm
Onions, chopped	2 tbsp / 50 gm
Ginger (*adrak*), chopped	1 tbsp / 24 gm
Green chillies, chopped	4-5
Yoghurt (*dahi*)	1/3 cup / 100 gm
Mango powder (*amchur*)	1 tsp / 2 gm
Sugar	1 tbsp / 20 gm
Salt to taste	
Rock salt (*kala namak*)	1 tsp / 4 gm

Method

1. Blend the mint leaves, green coriander, onions, ginger and green chillies to make a smooth paste. Keep aside.
2. In a mixing bowl, whisk the yoghurt with mango powder, sugar, salt and rock salt. Add the mint paste and mix well.
3. Serve with kebabs.

Nariyal Chutney

Prep. time: 30 min. • Cooking time: 5 min. • Serves: 4

Ingredients

Coconut (*nariyal*), grated	1 cup / 240 gm
Green chillies, chopped	2-3
Ginger (*adrak*), chopped	1 tsp / 10 gm
Split black gram (*urad dal*), roasted	1 tbsp / 15 gm
Salt to taste	
For the tempering:	
Vegetable oil	4 tsp / 20 ml
Dry red chillies (*sookhi lal mirch*)	5
Mustard seeds (*rai*)	½ tsp / 1 gm

Method

1. Blend the coconut, green chillies, ginger and split black gram to a smooth paste. Add a little water, if required. Transfer into a bowl and mix in the salt.
2. **For the tempering**, heat the oil in a pan; add the dry red chillies and mustard seeds. Sauté till they crackle.
3. Remove from heat and mix it with the coconut paste.
4. Serve with any south Indian snacks.

Tomato chutney

Prep. time: 10 min. • Cooking time: 5 min. • Serves: 4

Ingredients

Tomatoes	335 gm
Ginger (*adrak*), chopped	1½ tsp / 15 gm
Red chilli powder	½ tsp / 1 gm
Coconut (*nariyal*), grated	5 tsp / 10 gm
For the tempering:	
Vegetable oil	2 tsp / 10 ml
Split black gram (*urad dal*)	1 tsp / 5 gm
Dry red chilli (*sookhi lal mirch*)	1
Mustard seeds (*rai*)	1 tsp / 3 gm

Method

1. Blanch the tomatoes in boiling water for a minute. Remove from heat and keep aside to cool.
2. Purée the tomatoes, ginger, red chilli powder and coconut together. Transfer to a serving bowl.
3. **For the tempering**, heat the oil in a pan; add the split black gram, dry red chilli and mustard seeds. Sauté till they crackle.
4. Remove from heat and pour this tempering over the prepared purée. Mix and serve with any dish.

Roasted gram flour chutney

Prep. time: 20 min. • Cooking time: 30 min. • Serves: 4

Ingredients

Gram flour (besan), roasted	1 cup / 100 gm
Water	½ cup / 100 ml
Salt to taste	
For the tempering:	
Vegetable oil	2 tsp / 10 ml
Mustard seeds (rai)	⅓ tsp / 1 gm
Curry leaves (kadhi patta)	1 sprig
Dry red chillies (sookhi lal mirch)	5

Method

1. Mix the gram flour with water to make a smooth paste. Add salt and mix well.
2. **For the tempering**, heat the oil in a pan; add the mustard seeds and sauté till it crackles. Add the curry leaves and dry red chillies. Stir and remove from heat. Pour this over the gram flour paste, mix and serve with any dish.

Rajasthani tangy relish

Prep. time: 30 min. • Cooking time: 30 min. • Serves: 4

Ingredients

Kachri*, ground	30 gm
Vegetable oil for frying	
Cumin (*jeera*) seeds, powdered	1 tsp / 2 gm
Garlic (*lasan*), ground	100 gm
Onion, medium-sized, chopped	1
Dry red chillies (*sookhi lal mirch*), ground	4-5
Yoghurt (*dahi*)	½ cup / 90 gm
Salt to taste	

Method

1. Heat 1 tsp oil in a pan; add the cumin seeds and garlic. Sauté for a few seconds.
2. Add the onion and fry till brown. Add the remaining ingredients and cook on a low flame till the oil separates. Remove from the fire and keep aside to cool.
3. When cool, store in an airtight jar. If refrigerated, this chutney will stay for a month.

Note: Kachri is a sour, cucumber-like vegetable from the melon family. It is sliced and stored in dried form and imparts a tanginess to the dishes.

Rajasthani garlic relish

Prep. time: 30 min. • Serves: 4

Ingredients

Garlic (*lasan*), skinned	100 gm
Cumin (*jeera*) seeds	1 tsp / 2 gm
Red chilli powder	2-3 tsp / 4-6 gm
Yoghurt (*dahi*)	¼ cup / 45 gm
Salt to taste	

Method

1. Combine all the ingredients together and blend to a smooth paste.
2. Store in an airtight jar until ready to use. If refrigerated, this chutney will easily stay for 2 weeks.

Smell-free

To remove the smell of garlic from your hands, rub coffee powder or lemon juice and wash with soap.

Rajasthani mango relish

Prep. time: 30 min. ● Cooking time: 30 min. ● Serves: 4

Ingredients

Mangoes, raw, unpeeled, cut into pieces	700 gm
Mustard (*sarson*) oil	½ cup / 85 ml
Panch phoran (see p. 8)	1 tsp / 3 gm
Red chilli powder to taste	
Salt to taste	
Turmeric (*haldi*) powder	½ tsp / 1 gm
Coriander (*dhaniya*) powder	1½ tsp / 2 gm
Water	½ cup / 100 ml
Jaggery (*gur*)	¾ cup / 150 gm

Method

1. Heat the oil in a wok (*kadhai*); add the *panch phoran*. When it crackles, add all the ingredients (except water and jaggery). Sprinkle 2-3 tbsp water and cook covered for 5-7 minutes.
2. When the mangoes soften a little, add the jaggery and ½ cup water. Cook till tender.
3. Remove and serve.

Rajasthani tomato relish

Prep. time: 15 min. ● Cooking time: 15 min. ● Serves: 4

Ingredients

Tomatoes, chopped	750 gm
Vegetable oil	2 tbsp / 30 ml
Panch phoran (see p. 8)	1 tsp / 3 gm
Green chillies, slit	2
Red chilli powder to taste	
Salt to taste	
Turmeric (*haldi*) powder	½ tsp / 1 gm
Coriander (*dhaniya*) powder	1 tsp / 2 gm
Sugar	4 tbsp / 80 gm

Method

1. Heat the oil in a wok (*kadhai*); add the *panch phoran* and when it crackles, add the remaining ingredients (except sugar). Mix well and cook covered on a low flame for 7 minutes.

2. Add the sugar and cook till a gravy-like consistency is reached. Serve cold.

Kashmiri walnut chutney

Prep. time: 15 min. • Serves: 8-10

Ingredients

Walnuts (*akhrot*), without shells	100 gm
Onions, chopped	½ cup / 120 gm
Green chillies, chopped	2
Yoghurt (*dahi*)	½ cup / 90 gm
Red chilli powder	½ tsp / 1 gm
Salt to taste	

Method

1. Grind the onions and green chillies together to a smooth paste. Add the walnuts and grind again for 30-40 seconds.
2. Transfer the mixture into a bowl. Mix in the yoghurt, red chilli powder and salt. Serve.

Pickle Power

*Stuff bittergourds, okra, etc.,
with leftover pickle masala, the
vegetables will have a tangy and
an unusual flavour.*

Green chilli chutney

Prep. time: 15 min. • Serves: 4-6

Ingredients

Green chillies, diced	100 gm
Salt to taste	
Water	2 tsp / 10 ml
Yoghurt (*dahi*), optional	1 tsp / 15 gm

Method

1. Grind the green chillies and salt with water into a coarse paste. Remove the lid of the grinder carefully or your eyes will sting.
2. Mix in the yoghurt, if desired and serve.

Longer Lasting
After refilling a pickle container, rub salt on the mouth of the container to prevent the pickle from spoiling.

Kashmiri radish chutney

Prep. time: 20 min. • Serves: 4-6.

Ingredients

Radish (*mooli*), scraped, grated	150 gm
Yoghurt (*dahi*), whisked	1 cup / 180 gm
Salt to taste	
Red chilli powder	½ tsp / 1 gm

Method

1. Squeeze the radish with both your hands and then keep in a serving bowl.
2. Add the yoghurt, salt and red chilli powder. Mix and serve.

Muji Chetin

Pickle Remedy

Remove fungus from pickles by adding 10-12 drops of acetic acid. Then store the pickle in a clean jar.

Kashmiri fried radish chutney

Prep. time: 10 min. • Cooking time: 10 min. • Serves: 6-8

Ingredients

White radish (*safed mooli*), grated	500 gm
Vegetable oil	4 tbsp / 40 ml
Carom (*ajwain*) seeds	½ tsp / 1 gm
Cumin (*jeera*) seeds	½ tsp / 1 gm
Salt to taste	
Asafoetida (*hing*)	a pinch
Turmeric (*haldi*) powder	½ tsp / 1 gm
Ginger powder (*sonth*)	½ tsp / 1 gm
Aniseed (*moti saunf*) powder	½ tsp / 1 gm
Red chilli powder (optional)	½ tsp / 1 gm
Green chilli, chopped	1
Juice of lemon (*nimbu*)	1
Walnuts (*akhrot*), crushed	50 gm

Method

1. Heat the oil in a pan; add the carom seeds, cumin seeds, salt and asafoetida. Stir for 30 seconds, then add the radish. Cook over a medium flame till the water evaporates and the oil separates.
2. Add the turmeric powder, ginger powder, aniseed powder, red chilli powder, green chilli and lemon juice. Cook for about 5 minutes, then add the walnuts.
3. Remove and serve at room temperature.

Tomato Khajoor Chutney

Bengali tomato and date chutney

Prep. time: 20 min. • Cooking time: 30 min. • Serves: 4

Ingredients

Tomatoes, chopped	1 kg
Dates (khajur), deseeded	½ cup / 25 gm
Vegetable oil	2 tsp / 10 ml
Mustard seeds (rai)	1 tsp / 2 gm
Dry red chillies (sookhi lal mirch)	2
Sugar	½ cup / 75 gm
Salt to taste	

Method

1. Heat the oil; add the mustard seeds and dry red chillies. Sauté for a few seconds, till the mustard seeds start crackling.
2. Add the tomatoes and cook for 15 minutes. Add the sugar and salt, stir till the sugar dissolves.
3. Cook till the mixture thickens. Lastly, mix in the dates. Keep aside to cool.
4. Serve at room temperature. When refrigerated, this chutney can stay for 2-3 days.

Garlic poppadoms

Prep. time: 24 hrs. • Serves: 4

Ingredients

Split black gram (*urad dal*) flour	200 gm
Garlic (*lasan*), chopped	2½ tbsp / 30 gm
Green chillies, chopped	4-5
Salt to taste	
Yellow chilli powder	1 tsp / 2 gm
Vegetable oil	2 tbsp / 20 ml
Water	1¼ cups / 250 ml

Method

1. Mix the split black gram flour, garlic, green chillies, salt, yellow chilli powder and oil together. Add water and knead to a stiff dough.
2. Divide the dough into small, even-sized balls (around 30) and roll each out into very thin discs.
3. Spread them out on a clean sheet and keep them in the sun to dry for a day or two.
4. Serve roasted or fried with any meal.

A sweet and sour relish

Prep. time: 10 min. • Cooking time: 20 min. • Serves: 4

Ingredients

Dry mango powder (*amchur*)	5 tsp / 10 gm
Black pepper (*kali mirch*) powder	½ tsp / 1 gm
Rock salt (*kala namak*), powdered	½ tsp / 2 gm
Garam masala (see p. 8)	½ tsp / 1 gm
Ginger powder (*sonth*)	½ tsp / 1 gm
Red chilli powder	½ tsp / 1 gm
Salt to taste	
Sugar	5 tbsp / 100 gm
Raisins (*kishmish*), clean, washed	2 tsp / 10 gm

Method

1. Mix all the ingredients (except raisins) with ½ cup water in a saucepan and cook gently for 15 minutes. Ensure that the mixture is lump-free and the sugar dissolves completely. Add the raisins.

2. Serve with *dahi vadas*, *papri chaat*, and so forth.

Prep. time: 7 days. ● Cooking time: 20 min. ● Serves: 4

Ingredients

Cauliflower (*phool gobhi*), cut into florets	500 gm
Turnips (*shalgam*), thinly sliced	300 gm
Carrots (*gajar*), thinly sliced	300 gm
Mustard (*sarson*) oil	2 cups / 350 ml
Onions, puréed	100 gm
Ginger-garlic (*adrak-lasan*) paste	5 tbsp / 105 gm
Sugar	¾ cup / 112 gm
Vinegar (*sirka*)	1 cup / 200 ml
Garam masala (see p. 8)	5 tsp / 10 gm
Red chilli powder	4 tsp / 8 gm
Cumin (*jeera*) seeds	4 tsp / 8 gm
Mustard seeds (*rai*)	4 tsp / 8 gm
Salt to taste	

Method

1. Keep the vegetables in the sun to dry for 2 days.
2. Heat the mustard oil in a wok (*kadhai*); add the onion purée and ginger-garlic paste, stir-fry for a few minutes. Add the dry spices, salt and the vegetables. Cook covered for 5-10 minutes.
3. Mix the sugar in the vinegar, stir till the sugar dissolves completely. Add this mixture to the vegetables and mix well. Remove, keep aside to cool. Transfer the contents into a glass jar, cover with a cloth and secure with a string. Keep in the sun for 5 days. Serve with any meal.

Nepalese radish pickle

Prep. time: 5-6 hrs. • Serves: 2-4

Ingredients

Radish (*safed mooli*), peeled, washed	500 gm
Red mustard seeds (*lal rai*)	100 gm
Cumin (*jeera*) seeds	4 tsp / 8 gm
Timmur (see front cover flap), optional	½ tsp / 3 gm
Red chilli powder	4 tsp / 8 gm
Salt to taste	
Turmeric (*haldi*) powder	2 tsp / 4 gm
Mustard (*sarson*) oil	2 cups / 340 ml
Lemon (*nimbu*) juice	2 tsp / 10 ml

Method

1. Pat dry the radish and cut into 3"-long pieces. Cut each piece diagonally into four. Spread them on a flat dish and leave indoors for 5-6 hours.

2. Grind the red mustard seeds, cumin seeds and *timmur* to a coarse paste.

3. Mix the paste, salt and turmeric powder together. Add 2-3 tbsp oil and lemon juice. Mix well. Add the radish and rub the spice mixture well into the pieces.

4. In a dry glass jar, add the pieces, a few at a time. Press down after each addition to pack them well. Cover and put the jar out in the sun for 2 days. On the third day, shake the bottle well. There should be water in it. Add the remaining oil and mix well. It will be ready for consumption after 6-7 days.

Nepalese tomato relish

Prep. time: 15 min. • Cooking time: 20 min. • Serves: 2-4

Ingredients

Tomatoes, ripe, cut into 8 pieces	½ kg
Mustard (sarson) oil	4 tbsp / 40 ml
Fenugreek seeds (methi dana)	½ tsp / 1½ gm
Jimmu (see front cover flap), optional	½ tsp / 3 gm
Dry red chillies (sookhi lal mirch), halved, deseeded	2
Garlic (lasan), chopped	2 tsp / 6 gm
Ginger (adrak), julienned	2 tsp / 6 gm
Turmeric (haldi) powder	½ tsp / 1 gm
Salt to taste	
Cumin (jeera) seeds, dry roasted, powdered	1 tsp / 2 gm
Red chilli powder	½ tsp / 1 gm

Method

1. Heat the oil until smoking hot; lower the flame and temper with fenugreek seeds, jimmu and dry red chillies.

2. When the chillies turn brown, add the garlic and ginger. Once the garlic browns a little, add the tomatoes, turmeric powder and salt. Cook over a high flame stirring continuously, till the liquid gets absorbed.

3. Add the cumin seeds and red chilli powder. Stir occasionally and cook till the liquid dries and the oil separates.

4. Transfer into a jar and keep aside to cool. This can be refrigerated for up to one week.

Nepalese potato pickle

Prep. time: 20 min. • Cooking time: 15 min. • Serves: 2-4

Ingredients

Potatoes, preferably lemon-sized ones, boiled, peeled, halved	500 gm
Gingelly seeds (*safed til*)	2 tbsp / 10 gm
Cumin (*jeera*) seeds	1 tsp / 2 gm
Timmur (see front cover flap), optional	½ tsp / 3 gm
Salt to taste	
Juice of lemons (*nimbu*)	2
Mustard (*sarson*) oil	4 tbsp / 40 ml
Fenugreek seeds (*methi dana*)	½ tsp / 2 gm
Green chillies, split	5-6
Turmeric (*haldi*) powder	½ tsp / 1 gm
Green coriander (*hara dhaniya*), chopped	for garnishing

Method

1. Dry roast the gingelly seeds, cumin seeds and *timmur* in a pan. Grind together with a little water.
2. Mix the potatoes with the above paste, salt and lemon juice.
3. Heat the oil in a pan; add the fenugreek seeds. When it crackles, add the green chillies and cover for a minute. Remove the cover and add the turmeric powder. Pour this over the potatoes. Mix well.
4. Serve cold garnished with green coriander.

Kankro Achar

Prep. time: 20 min. • Serves: 2-4

Ingredients

Cucumber, cut into 2" pieces	500 gm
Gingelly seeds (safed til), dry roasted	1 tbsp / 5 gm
Cumin (jeera) seeds, dry roasted	1 tsp / 2 gm
Timmur (see front cover flap), roasted (optional)	6 grains
Yoghurt (dahi)	1 tsp / 5 gm
Salt to taste	
Mustard (sarson) oil	1 tbsp / 10 ml
Fenugreek seeds (methi dana)	¼ tsp / 1 gm
Jimmu (see front cover flap), optional	¼ tsp / 1½ gm
Green chillies, slit in 4, deseeded	2
Turmeric (haldi) powder	2 pinches
Red chilli powder	½ tsp / 1 gm
Green coriander (hara dhaniya), chopped	½ tsp / 1 gm

Method

1. Remove the cucumber seeds, mix in the salt.
2. Grind the gingelly seeds, cumin seeds and timmur together. Add the yoghurt and 2 tbsp water to make a paste. Add a little salt.
3. Squeeze the cucumber to remove the excess water. Rub well with the prepared paste.
4. Heat the oil in a pan; add the fenugreek seeds, jimmu and green chillies. Remove from the flame; mix in turmeric powder and red chilli powder. Pour this mixture over the cucumber. Mix well, adding 1-2 tsp water. Garnish with green coriander and serve cold.

Kashmiri kohlrabi pickle

Prep. time: 30 min. ● Serves: 2-4

Ingredients

Kohlrabi (*ganth gobhi*), only bulbs, washed	I kg
Mustard (*sarson*) oil	I¼ cups / 255 ml
Red chilli powder	3 tbsp / 9 gm
Ginger powder (*sonth*)	2 tsp / 4 gm
Asafoetida (*hing*)	¼ tsp / I¼ gm
Mustard seeds (*rai*)	3 tbsp / 18 gm
Carom (*ajwain*) seeds	I tsp / I½ gm
Salt to taste	

Method

1. Dry the kohlrabi with a soft cloth and cut the bulb into half. Make ¹/₃"-thick slices, without peeling. Dry these slices in the sun for 3-4 hours.

2. Heat half the oil, cool and then put aside. In the remaining oil, mix all the spices well with a wooden spoon. Add the kohlrabi. Mix well so that the slices are well coated with the paste.

3. Take a large, dry jar and put the spiced slices and any extra oil in the pot. Seal with a polyfilm and then cover the lid.

4. Keep this jar in the sun for 4-6 days (in winter) and 2-3 days (in summer). At first the level of oil will rise in the jar and will then settle down.

5. When the oil settles down, pour in the remaining oil so that the mixture is covered with oil. Keep in the sun for a few more days.

Desserts

Bengali flour crispies

Prep. time: 1 hr. • Cooking time: 1½ hrs. • Serves: 4-6

Ingredients

For the dough:

Refined flour (*maida*)	1 cup / 100 gm
Vegetable oil	2 tbsp / 20 gm
Saffron (*kesar*), soaked in 1 tbsp water	a few strands
Water	4 tbsp / 60 ml

For the filling:

Wholemilk fudge (*khoya*), mashed	³/₅ cup / 65 gm
Almonds (*badam*), slivered	2 tbsp / 30 gm
Pistachios (*pista*), slivered	2 tbsp / 30 gm
Cloves (*laung*), powdered	½ tsp / 1gm
Sugar, powdered	2 tbsp / 40 gm

For the sugar syrup:

Sugar	3 cups / 450 gm
Water	3½ cups / 700 ml

Cloves (*laung*)	12
Vegetable oil for frying	

Method

1. Sieve the flour and make a well in the centre.
2. Add the oil and saffron, mix well. Add water gradually, and knead to make a hard dough. Cover the dough with a moist cloth and keep aside for 15 minutes.
3. **For the filling**, mix the wholemilk fudge, almonds, pistachios, clove powder and sugar together. Divide the filling into 12 equal portions.

4. **For the sugar syrup**, boil the water with sugar till the sugar dissolves completely. Then simmer for 2-3 minutes.

5. Divide the dough into 12 equal portions and shape each portion into balls. Roll out each ball into 6"-diameter pancakes.

6. Place one portion of the filling in the centre of each pancake and brush the edges with water. Fold the pancakes from one side to the centre and press firmly to seal in the filling. Repeat from the other side, to give a 2" -wide strip.

7. Keeping the folded side out, bring the two ends together to make a ring with the strip. Brush the edges with water and press them firmly down to the centre to form squares. Secure each square with a clove.

8. Heat the oil in a wok (*kadhai*); shallow fry the squares on low heat till crisp and golden brown Remove with a slotted spoon and drain the excess oil on absorbent kitchen towels.

9. Submerge these crispies in hot sugar syrup completely, turning gently. If required, soak for 2-3 minutes. Remove and drain the excess syrup.

10. Arrange neatly on a serving dish and serve.

Gram flour balls

Prep. time: 10 min. • Cooking time: 20 min. • Makes: 24

Ingredients

Gram flour (*besan*), sifted	2 cups / 200 gm
Ghee	¾ cup / 145 gm
Coconut (*nariyal*), dried, grated	2 tbsp / 30 gm
Walnuts (*badam*), chopped	2 tbsp / 30 gm
Nutmeg (*jaiphal*), ground	a pinch
Sugar	¾ cup / 110 gm

Method

1. Melt the ghee in a heavy-bottomed pan over moderately low heat. Add the gram flour, coconut, walnuts (keep some aside for garnishing) and nutmeg. Cook for 5 minutes, stirring constantly.
2. Add the sugar and continue to cook for 10-15 minutes or until the mixture is thick and golden brown.
3. Transfer the mixture to a clean, flat surface. When cool enough to handle, shape into 24 equal-sized balls.
4. Garnish with the remaining coconut and walnuts and serve. (You can store these for 10-15 days.)

Besan Ladoo

Nepalese sweetmeat

Bambaison

Prep. time: 15 min. • Cooking time: 30 min. • Serves: 2-4

Ingredients

Wholemilk fudge (*khoya*), grated	I kg
Ghee, unmelted	¾ cup / 145 gm
Sugar	1¼ cups / 187 gm
Milk	½ cup / 90 ml
Green cardamom (*choti elaichi*) powder	I tsp / 2 gm

Method

1. Heat the ghee in a heavy-bottomed pan. Add the wholemilk fudge and cook over a medium flame, stirring continuously till it is light golden in colour.

2. Add the sugar and milk; continue stirring till the sugar dissolves. Cook over a medium flame till the wholemilk fudge becomes a lumpy mass and leaves the sides of the pan.

3. Remove from the flame and mix in the green cardamom powder. Grease a flat plate with ghee and transfer the cooked lump on to it. Spread it out with a greased spatula or the back of a serving spoon. Cut into pieces when still hot. Remove from the plate only when it cools.

- 239 -

Nepalese rice flour delicacy

Prep. time: 20 min. • Cooking time: 20 min. • Serves: 2-4

Ingredients

Rice flour, finely ground	2 cups / 400 gm
Sugar	1 cup / 150 gm
Lemon (*nimbu*) juice	4 tsp / 20 ml
Gingelly seeds (*safed til*)	½ cup
Ghee	1¼ cups / 240 gm

Method

1. Mix together the rice flour, sugar and lemon juice. Collect in a heap, cover with a deep dish turned upside down. Keep aside for 4-5 hours. Remove the dish, and knead the mixture into a dough with a little water.
2. Sprinkle the gingelly seeds on a flat steel plate.
3. Make small lemon-sized balls of the dough and roll on the gingelly seeds. With your fingers press the balls to form flat rounds, about 5" diameter.
4. Heat some ghee in a flat pan; fry the rice rounds, with the gingelly seeds on top, till they become light brown. Keep spooning the ghee (from the pan itself) over the rounds, but do not turn them over. Remove with a slotted spoon and drain on absorbent kitchen towels.

Fried green gram pudding

Prep. time: 40 min. • Cooking time: 20 min. • Serves: 4

Ingredients

Split green gram (*moong dal*), soaked for 30 minutes	½ cup / 80 gm
Ghee	2 tbsp / 30 gm
Sugar	¼ cup / 37 gm
Water	½ cup / 100 ml
Green cardamoms (*choti elaichi*)	2
Cashew nuts (*kaju*), broken	2 tsp / 10 gm
Wholemilk fudge (*khoya*), fresh, grated	½ cup / 60 gm
Pistachios (*pista*), chopped	10

Method

1. Drain the split green gram and grind into a rough paste.
2. Heat the ghee in a wok (*kadhai*); fry the green gram paste till light golden in colour.
3. Bring the sugar and water to the boil in another pan. Stir continuously till the sugar dissolves completely. Boil rapidly for 5 minutes. Add to the fried paste.
4. Cook, stirring vigorously, till the mixture becomes thick. Add the green cardamom powder.
5. Garnish with cashew nuts, wholemilk fudge and pistachios. Serve hot.

Shredded carrot pudding

Prep. time: 40 min. • Cooking time: 1 hr. • Serves: 10-12

Ingredients

Carrots (*gajar*), washed, peeled, shredded	1 kg
Milk	2½ cups / 450 ml
Sugar	½ cup / 75 gm
Brown sugar	½ cup / 85 gm
Green cardamom (*choti elaichi*) powder	1 tsp / 1½ gm
Ghee	⅓ cup / 60 gm
Almonds (*badam*), slivered	2 tbsp / 30 gm
Raisins (*kishmish*)	2½ tbsp / 25 gm
Walnuts (*akhrot*), chopped	2½ tbsp / 40 gm
Cloves (*laung*), ground	½ tsp / 1 gm
Nutmeg (*jaiphal*), ground	½ tsp / 1 gm
Cinnamon (*dalchini*), ground	½ tsp / 1 gm

Method

1. Boil the carrots and milk in a pan. Reduce heat to moderate and cook for 20-25 minutes, stirring continuously, till the mixture is nearly dry.
2. Add both the sugars and half of the green cardamom powder, stirring continuously for 10-12 minutes. Remove and keep aside.
3. Heat the ghee in a pan over moderate heat; fry the almonds until golden. Add the carrot mixture, raisins, walnuts and ground spices. Cook till the mixture begins to separate from the sides.
4. Serve hot garnished with the remaining green cardamom powder.

Badam ka Halwa

Prep. time: 30 min. • Cooking time: 30 min. • Serves: 4-5

Ingredients

Almonds (*badam*), blanched, chopped	500 gm
Ghee	1 cup / 190 gm
Milk	1 cup / 180 ml
Sugar	3 cups / 450 gm
Green cardamom (*choti elaichi*) powder	1 tsp / 2 gm
Saffron (*kesar*)	a few strands
Silver leaf (*varq*), optional	

Method

1. In a food processor, grind the almonds with a little milk to make a fine paste.
2. Heat the ghee in a heavy-bottomed pan. Add the almond paste and cook over medium heat until light golden.
3. Add the milk and sugar, cook over medium heat for 10-15 minutes till the moisture evaporates and the mixture becomes thick. Remove from heat. Add the green cardamom powder and saffron.
4. To serve cold, spread on a greased tray, cut into small squares and decorate with silver leaf. To serve hot, ladle individual portions on to dessert plates and decorate with silver leaf.

Shallow fried pancakes served with thickened milk

Prep. time: 1½ hrs. • Cooking time: 1 hrs. • Serves: 4

Ingredients

For the sugar syrup:

Water	1¼ cups / 250 ml
Sugar	1 cup / 150 gm

For the batter:

Refined flour (*maida*)	2½ cups / 250 gm
Baking powder	½ tsp / 1gm
Yoghurt (*dahi*)	⅓ cup / 60 gm
Green cardamom (*choti elaichi*) powder	1 tsp / 2 gm
Saffron (*kesar*), soaked in 1 tbsp milk	a few strands
Ghee	1½ cups / 285 gm

For the thickened milk (*rabri*):

Milk	16½ cups / 3 lt
Sugar	1½ cups / 225 gm
Rose water (*gulab jal*)	5 drops
Pistachios (*pista*), chopped	20 gm

Method

1. **For the sugar syrup**, heat the water in a pan, add the sugar and cook till it reaches a thread-like consistency. Reduce heat.
2. Sieve the refined flour and baking powder in a mixing bowl. Add the other ingredients (except ghee) and enough water to make a batter of pouring consistency. Add milk, if required.
3. Heat the ghee in a flat pan; drop a spoonful of batter

and fry both sides till golden brown. Remove with a slotted spoon and drain the excess oil on absorbent kitchen towels. Repeat till all the batter is used up.

4. Dip the fried pancakes in the sugar syrup and remove immediately.

5. **For the thickened milk (*rabri*),** heat the milk in a heavy-bottomed pan; cook till it is reduced to $\frac{1}{3}$ rd. Stir in the remaining ingredients and remove from heat. Keep aside to cool and then refrigerate. Serve with the prepared pancakes.

Cleansing Milk

If the sugar used for making the syrup contains dirt, add a few spoonfuls of milk to the syrup. The dirt will float up by itself and you can take it out with a spoon.

Nepalese sweetened rice rings

Prep. time: 1 hr. ● Cooking time: 20 min. ● Serves: 4

Ingredients

Rice, soaked for 1 hour	1¼ cups / 250 gm
Cream (*malai*) or butter, fresh	1½ tbsp / 30 gm
Milk	½ cup / 90 ml
Jaggery (*gur*), ground	2½ tbsp / 50 gm
Water as required	
Vegetable oil or ghee for frying	

Method

1. Drain the rice and grind to a coarse paste.
2. Add the cream or butter, milk and jaggery and mix well.
3. Gradually, add water to the rice mixture to get a thin consistency. Keep aside for 15-20 minutes.
4. Heat the oil / ghee in a flat-bottomed pan. Place a medium-sized steel bowl upside down in the middle of the oil.
5. When the oil is smoking hot, take one ladleful of the batter and pour it slowly all around the bowl to make a ring. Alternatively, you can use a coconut shell with a hole to pour the batter.
6. Cook till brown; then turn and cook the other side too. The oil must be very hot and the ring should be turned quickly and removed from the oil as soon as it is done. Repeat till all the batter is used up.
7. Serve hot or cold.

Dry fruits in sugar syrup

Prep. time: 20 min. • Cooking time: 15 min. • Serves: 10-15

Ingredients

Cottage cheese (*paneer*), ½" cubes	250 gm
Ghee for frying	
Almonds (*badam*), blanched	½ cup / 60 gm
Raisins (*kishmish*)	½ cup / 50 gm
Coconut (*nariyal*), slivered	¼ cup / 60 gm
Dried dates (*khajoor*), deseeded, slivered	¼ cup / 12 gm
Black peppercorns (*sabut kali mirch*)	1 tsp / 2 gm
Water	1 cup / 200 ml
Sugar	1½ cups / 225 gm
Green cardamoms (*choti elaichi*), crushed	6
Saffron (*kesar*), soaked in 2 tsp hot water	a few strands
Candied sugar (*misri*)	¼ cup / 50 gm
Lemon (*nimbu*) juice	1 tbsp / 15 ml

Method

1. Heat the ghee in a wok (*kadhai*); fry the cottage cheese lightly. Remove, keep aside.
2. Heat 2 tbsp ghee in a pot. Lightly sauté the almonds, raisins, coconut, dried dates and black peppercorns for 1 minute.
3. Add water, sugar and green cardamoms. Stir till the water comes to the boil. Lower the flame and cook for 5 minutes. Add the soaked saffron.
4. Add the candied sugar and the lemon juice; stir again. When the syrup becomes thick but not dry, remove from heat and serve warm.

Sweetened Kashmiri rice

Prep. time: 15 min. • Cooking time: 30 min. • Serves: 4-6

Ingredients

Rice, Basmati, washed, soaked for 1 hour	1½ cups / 300 gm
Milk	5½ cups / 1 lt
Sugar	2 cups / 300 gm
Ghee	5 tbsp / 75 gm
Almonds (badam)	½ cup / 60 gm
Cashew nuts (kaju)	¼ cup / 30 gm
Raisins (kishmish)	¼ cup / 25 gm
Coconut (nariyal), diced	¼ cup / 60 gm
Cinnamon (dalchini), 1" sticks	3
Green cardamoms (choti elaichi)	6
Black peppercorns (sabut kali mirch)	6
Bay leaves (tej patta)	2
Saffron (kesar), soaked in ¼ cup water	2 gm
Cloves (laung)	6

Method

1. Heat the milk in a heavy-bottomed pan. Add the drained rice and cook on a low flame till the milk begins to get absorbed. Remove, keeping the rice a little under done. Transfer the rice to a flat dish. Add the sugar and mix well gently.

2. Heat the ghee in a heavy-bottomed pot. Lightly fry the dry fruits, coconut, cinnamon sticks, green cardamoms, black peppercorns and bay leaves.

3. Add the rice and the saffron water. Stir well.

4. Put a griddle (tawa) under the pot and cook covered, over a low flame till done. Serve garnished with cloves.

Sweet Rajasthani porridge

Prep. time: 15 min. • Cooking time: 30 min. • Serves: 4-6

Ingredients

Broken wheat (*dalia*)	200 gm
Ghee	½ cup / 95 gm
Aniseed (*moti saunf*)	I tsp / I½ gm
Almonds (*badam*), blanched, halved	8-10
Dry coconut (*copra*), slivers	I tbsp / 15 gm
Water	3 cups / 600 ml
Sugar	½ cup / 75 gm
Green cardamoms (*choti elaichi*), crushed	4

Method

1. Heat the ghee in a wok (*kadhai*); add the aniseed and let it crackle.
2. Add the broken wheat and stir-fry till it is well browned.
3. Add the almonds (keep a few aside for garnishing), dry coconut and water; bring to the boil. Lower the flame and cook till the broken wheat becomes tender.
4. Add the sugar and stir till it dissolves completely.
5. Remove from the flame, garnish with green cardamom and the remaining almonds.

Creamy almond-flavoured rice pudding

Badami Kheer

Prep. time: 30 min. • Cooking time: 30 min. • Serves: 4-5

Ingredients

Rice, long-grained, soaked for 30 minutes	½ cup / 100 gm
Almonds (*badam*), blanched, halved	½ cup / 60 gm
Full-cream milk	5½ cups / 1 lt
Green cardamom (*choti elaichi*) powder	2 tsp / 4 gm
Lemon (*nimbu*) rind, grated	1 tsp / 15 gm
Sugar	1 cup / 150 gm
Rose water (*gulab jal*)	4-5 drops
Cherries (*gilas*), optional	

Method

1. Boil the milk over medium heat. Add the rice, green cardamom powder and lemon rind. Cook until the rice is slightly over done.
2. Add the sugar and almonds and cook for 5-10 minutes, stirring from time to time with a wooden spoon. Cook till a thick consistency is obtained and is slightly golden in colour.
3. Add the rose water and garnish with cherries.
4. Serve hot or cold.

Richly garnished rice pudding

Prep. time: 30 min. ● Cooking time: 30 min. ● Serves: 4

Ingredients

Rice, Basmati, soaked in water for 30 minutes	60 gm
Milk	5½ cups / 1 lt
Sugar	1 cup / 150 gm
Saffron (*kesar*), soaked in 1 tbsp water	a few strands
Green cardamom (*choti elaichi*) powder	1 tsp / 2 gm
Rose water (*gulab jal*)	2 drops
Almonds (*badam*), slivered	¾ cup / 10 gm
Pistachios (*pista*), slivered	1 tsp / 5 gm
Silver leaf (*varq*) for garnishing	

Method

1. Drain the rice and blend to a smooth paste.
2. Heat the milk in a thick-bottomed pan and bring it to the boil. Stir in the rice paste and sugar and cook till the mixture thickens.
3. Add the saffron, green cardamom powder and rose water. Mix well and remove from heat. Keep aside to cool and then chill in a refrigerator.
4. Serve chilled garnished with almonds, pistachios and silver leaf.

Ice cream in earthenware moulds

Prep. time: 20 min. ● Cooking time: 2 hrs. ● Serves: 4

Ingredients

Milk	5½ cups / 1 lt
Sugar	4 tbsp / 80 gm
Saffron (kesar), soaked in 1 tbsp water	a few strands
Yellow colour	2-3 drops
Green cardamom (choti elaichi) powder	a pinch
Cashew nuts (kaju), chopped	1½ tbsp / 20 gm
Pistachios (pista), blanched, chopped	1 tbsp / 15 gm

Method

1. Heat the milk in a wok (kadhai); cook on medium heat, stirring constantly till it is reduced to ¼ th.
2. Remove the milk from heat and stir in the sugar till it is completely dissolved.
3. Mix in the saffron, yellow colour, green cardamom powder, cashew nuts and pistachios.
4. Fill the mixture into earthenware moulds (kujja), cover with lid and seal with any dough.
5. Place the moulds in the freezer for 1½ hours to allow the mixture to set.
6. Remove from the freezer, take off the lid and serve immediately with falooda (see p. 253).

Fresh cornflour vermicelli served with *kulfi*

Prep. time: 10 min. ● Cooking time: 20 min. ● Serves: 4

Ingredients

Water	2 cups / 400 ml
Cornflour	½ cup / 90 gm
Yellow colour (optional)	a few drops

Method

1. Mix the water and cornflour in a wok (*kadhai*) and stir thoroughly. Add the yellow colour.
2. Cook on low heat, stirring continuously, till the mixture thickens and becomes gelatinous. Remove from heat.
3. Pour into a falooda press and place over a container filled with cold water.
4. Press the mixture out into a platter in one continuous stream without stopping.
5. Store the falooda in the refrigerator and serve chilled, as an accompaniment with *kulfi* (see p. 252). If desired, you can flavour the *falooda* with Roohafza or vetiver or rose water.

Soft cottage cheese dumplings in sugar syrup

Prep. time: 1 hr. • Cooking time: 4½ hrs. • Serves: 6-8

Ingredients

Full-cream milk	8 cups / 1½ lt
Lemon (*nimbu*) juice	4 tbsp / 60 ml
Water	8 cups / 1600 ml
Sugar	10 cups / 1½ kg
Cornstarch, dissolved in 2 tbsp water	1 tbsp / 15 gm
Vetiver (*kewda*) essence	4-5 drops

Method

1. Boil the full-cream milk in a heavy-bottomed pan; reduce heat and add the lemon juice to curdle. Remove from heat and keep aside for 10 minutes.

2. Pour the cheese-whey mixture into a moist cheesecloth. Pick up the cheesecloth by the corners, twist it loosely just to seal the cheese inside and rinse under the tap for a few minutes. Hang the cloth for 20-30 minutes to allow the excess water to drain.

3. Meanwhile, boil the water and sugar in a pan until the sugar dissolves completely. Cook on high heat for 3-4 minutes; remove from heat and keep aside.

4. Remove the cheese on a clear work surface and crumble it repeatedly till it becomes fluffy and smooth.

5. Knead into a smooth dough and coat with a thin layer of oil on all sides. Divide the dough into 16 portions and shape each into smooth balls.

6. Reheat the sugar syrup, bring to the boil and slide in

the prepared balls. Increase the heat and boil continuously for about 20 minutes adding the dissolved cornstarch after 4 minutes of boiling.

7. Add ¼ cup water to maintain the consistency of the syrup. Pour the water carefully directly into the syrup and not on the balls. Remove from heat.

8. Let the syrup cool for about 10 minutes then sprinkle the vetiver essence. Leave the dumplings to soak in the sugar syrup at room temperature for at least 4 hours. Serve chilled or at room temperature with the syrup.

Fruitful Sugar
Store brown sugar and dry fruits together. The sugar stays soft and gets a fruity flavour.

Glossary of Cooking Terms

Batter: A mixture of flour, liquid and sometimes other ingredients of a thin, creamy consistency.

Blend: To mix together thoroughly two or more ingredients.

Broil: Dry roast the food items in a heavy-bottomed pan over low heat without using oil or water.

Curdle: To separate milk into curd and whey by acid or excessive heat.

Dough: A thick mixture of uncooked flour and liquid, often combined with other ingredients: the mixture can be handled as a solid mass.

Grind: To reduce hard food such as pulses, lentil, rice, and so forth, to a fine or coarse paste in a grinder or blender.

Purée: To press food through a fine sieve or blend it in a blender or food processor to a smooth, thick mixture.

Sauté: To cook in an open pan in hot, shallow fat, tossing the food to prevent it from sticking.

Skewer: Fasten together pieces of food compactly on a specially designed long pin, for cooking.

Steam: To cook food in steam. Generally food to be steamed is put in a perforated container which is placed above a pan of boiling water. The food should not come into contact with the water.

Stir: To mix with a circular action, usually with a spoon, fork or spatula.

Temper: Combine spices and flavourings with hot oil or ghee, and then pour this over the main preparation.